Lakeland Walking: on the level

Norman Buckley

Reprinted with revisions: 1995, 1997, 1998, 2000, 2003, 2008
Reprinted 2004, 2005, 2008

Published by Sigma Leisure – an imprint of
Sigma Press, Stobart House, Pontyclerc, Penybanc Road, Ammanford, Carmarthenshire SA18 3HP, UK

British Library Cataloguing in Publication Data
A CIP record for this book is available from the British Library

ISBN: 978-1-85058-389-9

Typesetting and Design by: Sigma Press, Ammanford, Carms.

Cover photograph: Woods near Hodge Close *(June Buckley)*

Printed by: Progress Press Ltd, Malta

Disclaimer: the information in this book is given in good faith and is believed to be correct at the time of publication. No responsibility is accepted by either the author or publisher for errors or omissions, or for any loss or injury howsoever caused. Only you can judge your own fitness, competence and experience. Do not rely solely on sketch maps for navigation: we strongly recommend the use of appropriate Ordnance Survey (or equivalent) maps.

PREFACE

Level-walks in England's highest and most concentrated mountain area! Whatever next - hill walking in East Anglia? But it really depends on what is meant by level. A purist interpretation would undoubtedly disqualify the great majority of the walks in this book, but setting the parameters a little more flexible permits the inclusion of a surprising number of more or less level routes, many of which are close to the high fells and all of which have scenic and/or other interesting features.

Love of the mountains and the desire to admire them at close quarters is by no means confined to those with the physical ability and the will-power to climb the long and often steep slopes which lead to high ground and, ultimately, the summits. Maybe anno domini or disability are taking their toll of once vigorous fell walkers, maybe an urban upbringing has induced deep mistrust and an exaggerated fear of the height, wildness, and danger of the mountains, maybe the need to exercise young children in safety is paramount. For whatever reason, good walks of varying length in mountain country, but which in themselves do not include significant climbing, will always be popular. Inevitably, some walks are more level than others and the strenuousness or otherwise of a route does not, of course, depend solely on the total ascent. The steepness of that ascent and whether it is all in one continuous slope or is divided into several short slopes with long level stretches in between, and the conditions underfoot, are all relevant. For these reasons, the introduction to each walk quantifies the distance and the ascent, and briefly describes the route in such a way that prospective walkers should be in no doubt as to the effort required and of the likely difficulty, if any.

Although by Lakeland standards these are mainly easy walks, the use of sturdy footwear, preferably boots, is strongly advised. Many low lying footpaths become muddy during and after rain, and a good, but stony, path will be uncomfortable to the feet through soles of inadequate thickness or rigidity. Proper shaping of the underside of the boot or shoe sole gives much improved adhesion on all surfaces and consequent confidence to the walker; smooth surfaced soles can be dangerous even on gently sloping grass.

Although even the longest of the walks can be completed in about $2^1/_2$ hours, it is likely that most walkers will prefer to proceed at a more leisurely pace, allowing time for full appreciation of scenery and features, and for refreshment. With this approach in mind, mention is made of hotels and other catering facilities; good picnic sites are also suggested.

Acknowledgement

The only acknowledgement appropriate to the writing of this book is to my wife, June. Having given up mountain walking, she has long insisted that there must be others who share her love of the Lake District scenery and wish to combine not too strenuous walking with the enjoyment of that scenery. The book is, inevitably, her idea. Indeed, the primary criterion for the inclusion of a walk has been whether or not June can complete it without difficulty and consequent complaint!

Norman Buckley

Contents

Location Map

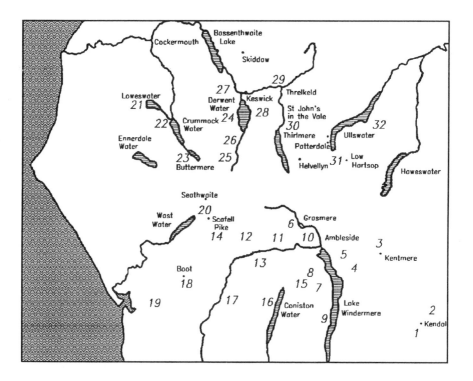

Italic numerals denote approximate locations of walks

1. Kendal

Walk: Scout Scar.

Length: Variable. 1 – 3 miles.

Rise and Fall: 150 feet approximately. Short but steep rise at start.

Underfoot: Good. Exceptionally dry.

Car Parking: Official free car park close to summit of Kendal to Underbarrow road. Grid reference – 493926.

Ordnance Survey: "English Lakes, South Eastern area" 1:25000.

Description

Scout Scar is a broad two mile long ridge running north-south and situated to the south-west of Kendal. Geologically it is part of the rim of the limestone which formerly covered the other various rocks of the Lake District. The limestone forms an impressive scarp along the west-facing side of the scar, with more gentle slopes down to Kendal on the east. Although the highest point is only 713 feet and the scar is very much on the edge of the district, it does make a very attractive easy walk, with great views of the high mountains to the north and west, and the Pennines to the east.

Scout Scar also has considerable botanical interest; beneath its apparently stunted ash and hawthorn trees is a rich assortment of lime loving plants, many of them absent from the Lake District proper, with some growing at the north-western limit of their range. In spring, violets and spotted orchids are common.

Route

The Underbarrow road climbs to the west out of Kendal from the town centre traffic lights. Close to the summit of this road, about 2 miles from the town, is a signposted car park in a disused quarry on the right. Cross the road, to go through an old metal gate opposite. A well-worn track climbs steeply, the rise being approximately 100 feet to the top of Scout Scar. This is the only appreciable ascent of the walk and it really is worth making the effort to reach Scout Scar's long flat top only a little way above.

Lakeland from Scout Scar

Once up, several versions of the path are apparent, all heading generally south along the top, and walkers may, and do, wander at will. It is suggested that keeping close to the top of the cliff will provide the finest views of the Lakeland mountains across the broad green meadows and woodlands of the Lyth Valley below. Ahead is the estuary of the Kent, sparking in sunshine, with the knoll of Arnside Knott beyond. Closer, and to the right is the long mound of Whitbarrow Scar, another portion of the limestone rim.

The distance to be walked is entirely optional; a round of $2^1/_4$ miles results from heading south until opposite the large farm of Barrowfield

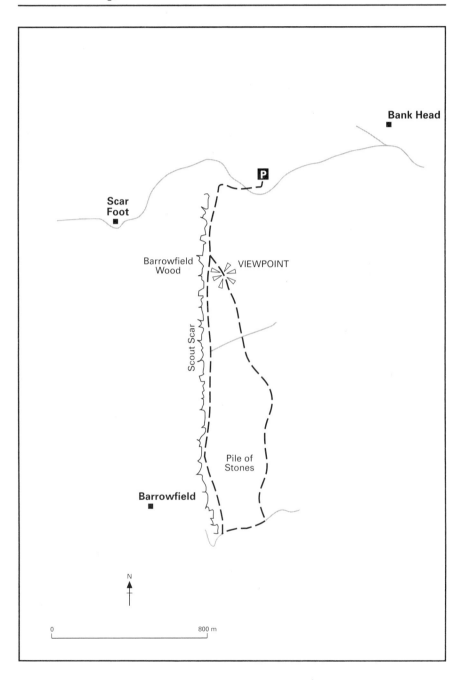

in the valley below, then turning left at a large stone cairn. A rise of about 50ft. reaches the crest of the ridge, where another left turn heads back towards the trig. point at the summit. The views to the right now include Ingleborough and the Howgill Fells above Sedbergh. From the trig. point the path carries on to the prominently situated shelter building, with its rather worn frieze setting out the highlights of the extensive view. The return to the car park is obvious.

2. Burneside

Walk: Burneside, Cowan Head and Bowston.

Length: 4 miles.

Rise and Fall: Less than 100 feet in total, well distributed. No steep gradients.

Underfoot: Very good. Some public road, but very little traffic.

Car Parking: Burneside – roadside spaces along Hall Road, a right turn from the village centre if the approach is from the Kendal direction. Grid reference: 506957.

Ordnance Survey: "English Lakes, South Eastern area" 1:25000.

Description

The Burneside area is not the first place which would come to mind when choosing a Lakeland walk. However, to the north-west of Kendal the broad valley of the R. Kent is not without a gentle pastoral charm and there are features which go some way to making up for the lack of real mountains, one being the peace and quiet when central Lakeland is overrun by visitors. Above all, the area has appeal for students of industrial history; for centuries the waters of the Kent were harnessed to power a great array of mills. From above Staveley down to Kendal itself generations of bobbin, textile and paper mills crowded the banks and produced weirs, ponds, and sluices in profusion to regulate the flow of water to their water-wheels. They also produced the reservoir at Kentdale Head (ref. Walk No. 3) to provide extra reserves in times of drought. An early (mid 18th century) paper mill was at Cowan Head, where the site has recently been converted into a residential complex. Together with mills at Bowston and Burneside, this mill became part of the paper business owned and operated by the Cropper family from the mid 19th century. Narrow gauge railway lines were constructed from the L.N.W.R. station at Burneside to the nearby mill and to the more distant mills at Bowston and Cowan Head. In 1927, the lines were converted to standard gauge and a petrol-engined locomotive was purchased to replace the horse power used on the narrow gauge predecessor. The small hamlet of Burneside was greatly enlarged by the provision of housing for the numerous mill employees. Only Burneside mill remains operational, still by Croppers, and the industrial railway lines have long been disused.

The now unmanned station at Burneside still has a passenger service and the walk may be started and finished at the station by following the main road towards Kendal, turning left a little way past the church into Hall Road, and joining the route beyond the paper factory.

Burneside Hall is a good example of a 14th century defensive pele tower, with a later manor house grafted on; the tower is in a sad state of dereliction.

Burneside Old Hall

Route

From Burneside, continue along Hall Road, crossing the R. Kent, passing various entrances to Cropper's factory, and soon reaching Burneside Hall. Turn left at the next road junction into a very minor road. In less than half a mile there are stiles on each side of the road.

Take the stile on the right and follow a little-used path beside a stream, heading for a stile at the far side of the field. Stay close to the wall, pass through a farm gate, and keep close to the foot of the knoll ahead, eventually bearing left to another farm gate. A lane now leads towards the three-storey Braban House. Cross the surfaced road by the drive entrance, turn right, cross a tiny stream and then 50 yards of meadow to a gate on the left. An old lane which is now a public bridleway leads to another minor road. Turn left at the road and then right at a road junction (a left turn here provides a quick route back to Bowston) following a "Staveley" signpost.

Reston Scar above Staveley fills the view ahead, doing its best to convince as a substitute for real mountains, as the road reaches Hagg Foot House in half a mile. At the far end of the building a public footpath sign points the way among the farm complex. Descend an unmade track relatively steeply to the river. From here there is a choice of path back to Bowston. On the far bank is the Dales Way, passing through Cowan Head, where there is still a weir, pond, and sluice gates, and then using the surfaced road for some of the distance, being careful to keep by the river at the point where the Cowan Head road turns right. On the near bank is a field edge track, avoiding all roadway until emerging close by Bowston Bridge.

Cross the bridge and go over the narrow stile immediately on the right. The Dales Way descends the stone steps and follows close to the river bank, fringed by good mature trees. The water in the Kent is now attractively clear, probably much more so than was the case in its industrial heyday. The paper factory comes into view and a ladder stile is reached.

The route goes ahead, either rising along the crest of the old river bank or, alternatively, keeping to its foot, with close views of the large stepped weir, which provided the large amount of water needed by the

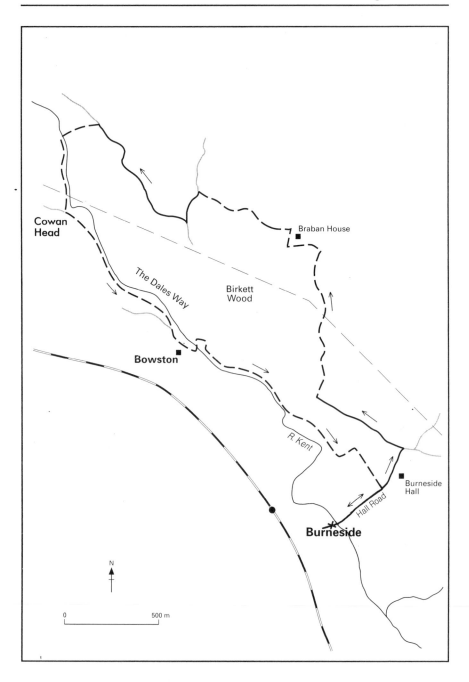

Cowan
Head

Braban House

The Dales Way

Birkett
Wood

Bowston

R. Kent

Burneside
Hall

Hall Road

Burneside

N

0   500 m

factory. More attractively, Burneside Hall again comes into view. The track goes round the edge of the factory site, quite well screened by tree planting, by a stile and a kissing gate, to reach Hall Road. Turn right to return to the village centre.

3. Kentmere

Walk: Kentmere circular.

Length: 5 miles.

Rise and Fall: Moderate. Total rise less than 300 feet. No steep gradients.

Underfoot: Generally very good. Some surfaced road, without traffic. 400 yards of rough footpath below reservoir – can be avoided.

Car Parking: At Kentmere church. Grid reference – 456041.

Ordnance Survey: "English Lakes, South Eastern area" 1:25000.

Description

Kentmere has always been regarded as one of Lakeland's quieter valleys, its entrance tucked away in the relatively unfashionable village of Staveley, now by-passed in the rush to reach more spectacular and congested central Lakeland. Nowadays, however, more walkers do seek out Kentmere's charms and the limited car park at the village church may well be inadequate at popular holiday periods.

The valley itself is a most pleasing combination of farming along the relatively narrow bottom, with increasingly wild fell sides above. Just one road serves the tiny village of Kentmere, with a short branch to the hamlet of Hallow Bank. Happily, the highway authority has resisted, or been unable to afford, any temptation to road improvement, and the $3^1/_2$ mile drive from Staveley must be taken at a speed which allows at least the passengers to enjoy the delightful scenery. Above Kentmere the valley sides become higher and wilder, culminating in the mountain amphitheatre of Yoke, Ill Bell, Froswick. Mardale Ill Bell and Harter Fell, around the steep valley head. In this setting the reservoir was formed in 1845/6 to regulate the water to the many mills, principally at Staveley and Burneside, which relied on the fast flowing R. Kent for their power. Long disused, it now adds significantly to the attraction of the scenery.

On foot the valley may be reached over mountain passes from adjacent valleys, the Nan Bield from Mardale and the Garburn Road from Troutbeck being particularly well-known. Within the valley several footpaths and bridleways provide good walking; the route described below gives a circular walk from Kentmere village of about 5 miles, around the upper part of the valley, with good mountain views, a pleasant half day excursion including a picnic by the reservoir.

Kentmere

Despite having the mainly 16th century church of St. Cuthbert and a village hall, Kentmere is a tiny community sitting at the head of the former valley lake, drained during the last century to provide extra land for farming. The village inn closed as long ago as 1887. A little way along the Garburn Road (trackway) is Kentmere Hall, a farm founded on a fine example of a 14th century defensive pele tower.

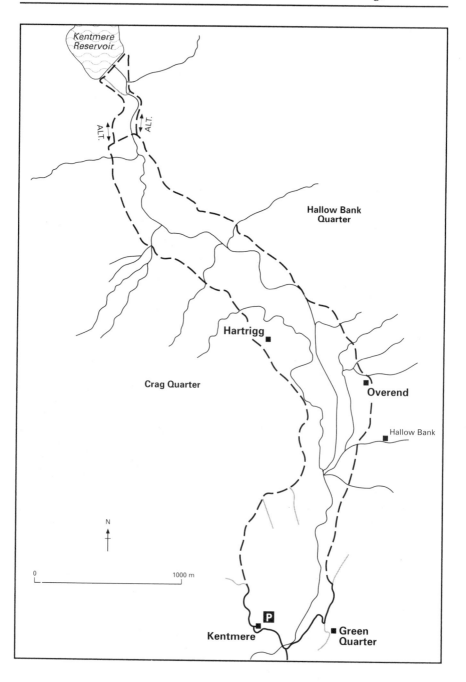

Route

From the small car park by the church carry on along the surfaced road, up and down but with no really prolonged ascent, and keeping right at a junction in less than a quarter of a mile. The little roadway passes close under the rocky spine which forms the south-east ridge of Yoke, passing Scales as it clings between the fellside and the farming land. Hartrigg, the highest farm in the valley, is reached at the end of the surfaced road. Take the gate on the left to by-pass the farm and follow a good wide trackway gently uphill and then down and round the foot of Rainsborrow Crag, which falls steeply from the summit of Yoke. Disused quarries are soon reached, beyond a series of glacial moraines in the valley bottom. At the quarries the river may be crossed for the return route on the east side of the valley.

Below: Kentmere

It would, however, be a pity not to visit the reservoir, only a a quarter of a mile or so further up the same trackway, with just the odd steep but very short pitch. Apart from the dam, the reservoir is in all other respects an attractive lake, well set among good mountain scenery. With a little agility the spillway can be crossed, at least in dry weather, and a rough, narrow, path can be followed downhill to return to the quarries. Otherwise, return along the roadway past Reservoir Cottage.

From the quarries a good path, easy underfoot, passes below Tongue Scar and through the yard of the ruined Tongue House, with the site of an ancient settlement behind. Although generally keeping above the valley bottom farm land, the track does at two points run very close to the river, giving the opportunity to admire a fine old stone bridge, of similar construction to Lakeland's celebrated pack-horse bridges. Across the valley the ridge with the three peaks of Yoke, Ill Bell and Froswick is very fine indeed. After passing Overend Farm, keep right to pass well below the hamlet of Hallow Bank, crossing a small footbridge over a tributary stream. The track enters a walled section angling upwards to join the surfaced road known as High lane. Turn right at the first road junction to return to the village and right again up to the church.

4. Windermere and Troutbeck

Walk: Moorhowe, Dubbs, and Longmire.

Length: 4 miles.

Rise and Fall: Total ascent 400 feet. No steep gradients.

Underfoot: Very good. Three-quarters of a mile on a quiet minor road.

Car Parking: Roadside spaces for a few cars close to the start of the walk at Moor Howe. Grid reference – 424006.

Ordnance Survey: "EnglishLakes, South Eastern area" 1:25000.

Description

Despite using named trackways, this circular walk is probably less well known that the great majority of the walks in this book. This comparative neglect has more to do with the absence of a lake or other feature of special interest than with any deficiency in the walk itself or any lack of good, extensive, views.

Route

Moor Howe is reached by car either from the main Kendal to Windermere road, taking the Troutbeck turning just on the Windermere side of Ings, or from the Windermere to Patterdale road by turning towards Ings and Kendal almost a mile south of Troutbeck church. Park close to the point where a wide, unsurfaced roadway (Dubbs road) leaves the public highway in a northerly direction.

Walk along this road, gently uphill, through prime Lakeland sheep farming country, divided by stone walls, passing a small plantation before reaching Dubbs reservoir, a pleasant but unremarkable small lake.

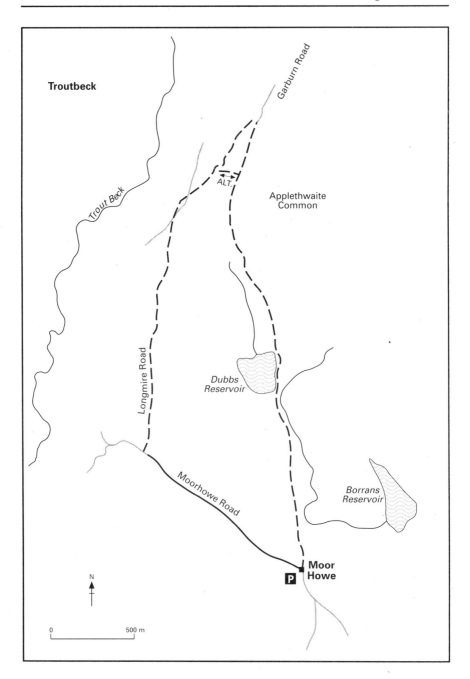

Troutbeck

Garburn Road

Trout Beck

ALT.

Applethwaite
Common

Longmire Road

Dubbs
Reservoir

Moorhowe Road

Borrans
Reservoir

Moor
Howe

P

N

0   500 m

Red Screes and the long ridge of Wansfell Pike show up well ahead. Soon there is a surprise view of the top end of Windermere and the Troutbeck valley, with the village strung out along the hillside opposite and much of the High Street range of mountains visible. Look very carefully for Thornthwaite Beacon on its lofty perch. Closely below and less attractive is the Limefitt Caravan Park, although it must be said that the tree screening is improving steadily and the site does appear to be well kept.

Dubbs Road

The track continues to a junction with the Garburn road, an old route over the ridge to Kentmere, but our way turns sharply to the left at this point. A short cut can be taken by going left over a stile 70 yards or so before a mixed woodland plantation and descending steeply across a field to reach the Garburn road by a ladder stile. The Garburn road is followed downhill, facing Windermere and Claiffe Heights beyond. A track joins on the right, followed by a left fork, uphill. This is now the Longmire road, heading south, with superb views to the Crinkle Crags,

Bowfell, Great End and the Coniston fells. If the visibility is good, Scafell and Scafell Pike may be seen peeping between the Crinkle Crags and Bowfell.

Turn left on reaching the Moor Howe road, signposted to Kendal via Ings, and return to the parking place.

5. *Troutbeck*

Walk: Troutbeck village.

Length: A little more than $2^1/_2$ miles.

Rise and Fall: Total ascent 150 ft. approx. Very gradual.

Underfoot: Good. Mostly on road – try to avoid peak periods.

Car Parking: Roadside area for a few cars 300 yards south of Townend on the Ambleside road. Grid reference – 406020.

Ordnance Survey: "English Lakes, South Eastern area" 1:25000.

Description

This is a walk with a difference; a gentle stroll along the street of Troutbeck village, with a return using back lanes for part of the way. Troutbeck is not really a village in any nucleated sense, but is a series of linked farming hamlets strung along one side of a broad valley. Below, on the main Windermere to Patterdale road, is the church of Jesus, much rebuilt and best known for its east window by Burne Jones, and the former school opposite. As the route of the walk is terraced well above valley floor level, the views across to the church and to the steep bare slopes of the Yoke, Ill Bell, and Froswick ridge are first rate, and the walk can be enjoyed for this alone.

But the real joy of this walk is in seeing at close quarters a remarkably fine and consistent selection of traditional Lakeland vernacular architecture. Houses, barns, and other outbuildings are strewn in profusion along the roadside, many easily seen without leaving the public highway. Most of the buildings are of agricultural origin and date from the 17th century, some having visible dates. Subsequent alterations and some Victorian "infill" houses have done little to spoil the harmony of this most attractive collection, With so many to choose from, space permits the mention of only a few examples under "Route", below.

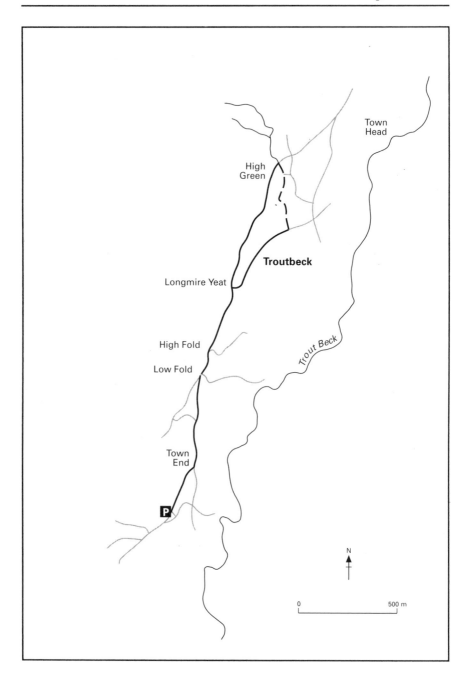

Route

From the car park turn right towards Troutbeck, passing Kilns, a cottage dated 1700, before reaching a road junction close to Town End. Possibly the most interesting house in the village, this is a "statesman's" (yeoman farmer) house. For generations the home of the Browne family, it is now owned by the National Trust and is open to the public during the holiday season. The house has most of the features expected in a 17th century farmhouse, but has been altered and extended over the years. Almost opposite is a fine example of a bank barn, still in agricultural use, as are most of Troutbeck's farm buildings. Unusually, the canopy over the barn doors has been extended to form a gallery. Don't miss the piece of old cruck framing which has been reused as a lintel over the door to the north end extension. Shortly, on the right, below road level, look out for a large and obviously very old house which has long been neglected, visible behind an "L" shaped barn.

Troutbeck

The village post office, offering cups of tea and coffee, and institute are reached at the next road junction, with the "Spinnery" opposite having a gallery tucked away round the corner. As progress is made along the road, the hamlet at High Fold, with its little walled green, is passed, then above to the left is a remarkable renovation of a long derelict house. The first and second "wells", those of St. John and St. James follow, then comes the hamlet of Longmire Yeat, followed by St. Margaret's well and a very long barn opposite with unusual features such as a hipped end to the roof and a chimney stack. A comparatively rare Edward VII post box is set in the far end wall of a Victorian house a little way before reaching the Mortal Man Inn, established in 1689 but totally rebuilt in the late 19th century. The well-known sign reads

"O mortal man that lives by bread, what is it makes thy nose so red,
     thou silly fool that looks so pale,
"tis drinking Sally Birkett's ale."

Town End, Troutbeck

The road continues to a cottage and a good bank barn; from this point the road rises and continues to Town Head, the northern extremity of the village. However, to return to the start, turn right on to a public bridleway by Scot Beck Fold, bear right at a junction, and descend steeply to High Green hamlet, opposite the Mortal Man. Turn left before the inn on to a roughly surfaced lane, and then right at a "village" signpost to follow an unsurfaced lane across the beck, rising a little to rejoin the outward route by "Myley Ghyll", and turning left to return to the car park.

6. Grasmere

Walk: White Moss Common to Grasmere.

Length: 1 mile.

Rise and Fall: Very little. Total rise 50 – 60 feet. No steep gradients.

Underfoot: Very good.

Car Parking: White Moss Common – large National Trust car parks on each side of the Ambleside to Grasmere road. Grid reference – 350065.

Ordnance Survey: "English Lakes, South Eastern area" 1:25000.

Description

The area surrounding the lakes of Grasmere and Rydal Water is an extremely attractive example of the magical combination of water, woodland, and fellside which is so typical of Lakeland at its best. The proximity of the villages of Grasmere and Rydal adds interest to the landscape, not least because of the strong literary associations. William Wordsworth spent his youthful years at Dove Cottage, Grasmere, and his last 37 years at Rydal Mount; the bank of daffodils at Dora's field, behind Rydal church can still be admired each spring. Both of his houses are open to the public.

Since large scale car parking was provided, the short section of river between the two lakes has become a great family favourite for picnics, paddling, and general recreation. Probably the finest spot of all is the small shingle beach at the foot of Grasmere, which is the destination of this walk, and from where lake swimming is possible.

Footbridge at White Moss

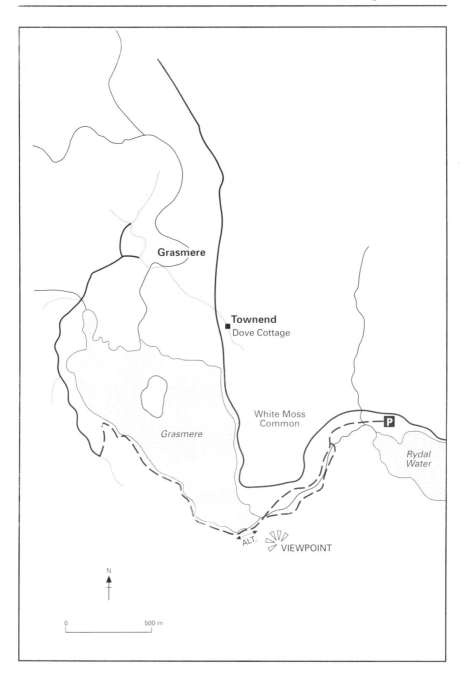

Route

The basic walk could hardly be more straightforward. From the car park on the south side of the road, set off on a broad level track parallel with the river. From the other car-park, cross the road and follow an obvious track leading towards the river. After the tracks join together, a curving footbridge over the river is soon reached. Cross this bridge and turn right. At this point a sign offers the choice of rising through the woodland to a viewpoint or of turning left to the Wetland Conservation Area (liable to flooding). The well-made path towards Grasmere clings to the steep hillside by the river, rising and falling just a little before reaching the foot of the lake, where the view opens up superbly, with Helm Crag sitting over the village and the head of the lake and looking more impressive than its modest height of 1299 feet (398m)

Helm Crag and Grasmere

(From the shingle beach the walk can be continued on a good path along the lake shore for a further three quarters of a mile, returning by the same route. Alternatively, a left turn at the far end of this track rises approx. 70 feet in 200 yards to reach the Elterwater to Grasmere minor road. Turn right to walk to Grasmere village in one mile for the bus back to White Moss car park.)

To return on foot from the shingle beach, cross the river by the footbridge and bear right to ascend the four steps and the gentle rise above before dropping to river level on a good broad track leading to the end of the first bridge, and retracing steps to the car park.

7. Windermere

Walk: Windermere lake shore.

Length: 2¹/₂ miles.

Rise and Fall: Negligible.

Underfoot: Excellent.

Car Parking: Red Nab car park. Grid reference - 385995.

Ordnance Survey: "English Lakes, South Eastern area" 1:25000.

Description

From the Ambleside to Hawkshead road, a lane meanders past the impressive entrance to Wray Castle, through High Wray hamlet and Claiffe Estate woodland to reach the small car park at Red Nab by the lake shore. Despite over-use, abuse, and the weight of tourism generally, Windermere remains a most attractive lake, seen at its best in the early morning or late evening light. The present walk is a very gentle amble along a largely wooded shore with views across the lake to mountains near and far, Wansfell Pike above Ambleside being prominent. Also across the lake is a good range of human activity, both past and present. The ancient Calgarth Hall is directly across from Red Nab, whilst a little further north White Cross Bay, now backed by a large but fortunately discreet caravan site, was once a hive of industry. During World War II Short Bros. operated a factory producing the giant Sunderland flying boats. Beyond Ecclerigg Crag is Brockhole, the National Park Visitor Centre, set in extensive and well laid out gardens and with its own lake jetty, followed by the Langdale Chase Hotel and the very prominent Low Wood Hotel.

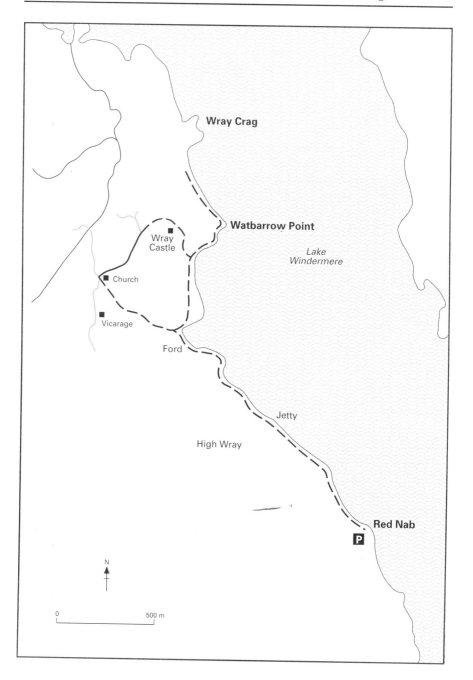

Route

From the car park turn left and follow the lake shore to the north along a good wide track. The route is entirely straightforward, mainly through the mixed woodland of the Claiffe Estate, and is always close to the water, passing Pinstone point, Wood Close Point, Epley Point and several traditional stone built boat-houses on the way. At High Wray Bay a lane rises gently to the left. Follow this for 50 yards or so to reach a stile which provides an ingenious passage for (small) dogs - or could it be used as a guillotine for four footed pests? A footpath leads invitingly along the now grassy shore and for those avoiding uphill walking this superb picnic/recreation area must be the destination of the walk, returning by the same route.

Windermere, shore footpath

(However, Wray Castle sits on the knoll above and a short, sharp, ascent of less than 100 feet is required to reach this Victorian sham, owned by the National Trust, not in itself particularly attractive, but a fine viewpoint. From the castle, the access drive can be followed to reach the public road, turning left and then left again almost immediately to return to High Wray Bay along the lane previously mentioned. Another extra option for walkers who can manage some ascent and descent is to continue from the grassy area, taking the path through the woods below the castle, to reach Wadbarrow Point, a substantial rocky outcrop pushing into the lake. A little way further is Low Wray Bay, with the huge Wray Castle boat-house and a public landing jetty.)

8. Blelham Tarn

Walk: Blelham Tarn and Outgate.

Length: $3^1/_4$ miles.

Rise and Fall: 260 feet in total. No really steep gradients.

Underfoot: Very varied, mostly good. Half a mile on very quiet minor road. A quarter of a mile on the Ambleside – Hawkshead road.

Car Parking: There are roadside spaces immediately to the south of the Wray Castle gate-house. Grid reference – 372007.

Ordnance Survey: "English Lakes, South Eastern area" 1:25000.

Description

This walk could well be a candidate for any collection claiming to be "off the beaten track in Lakeland". Despite, or perhaps because of its comparative neglect by visitors, Blelham Tarn is attractive in a gentle way. Because it is surrounded by farming land, its waters are unusually rich (eutrophic) for the district, producing algal blooms from time to time. Consequently, there are signs warning against drinking, bathing, or allowing dogs access to the water. The recommended circuit keeps quite well away from the shore of the lake.

The immediate countryside is a good mixture of meadow and woodland, much of it owned by the National Trust, while there are longer views to the mountains for much of the way. Outgate forms a convenient half-way point with its well-known inn serving bar food, open from 12 noon until 3 p.m. daily (and, of course, in the evenings).

Route

To reach the car parking area, leave Ambleside by the Skelwith Bridge/ Coniston road, turn left at Clappersgate towards Hawkshead, and then

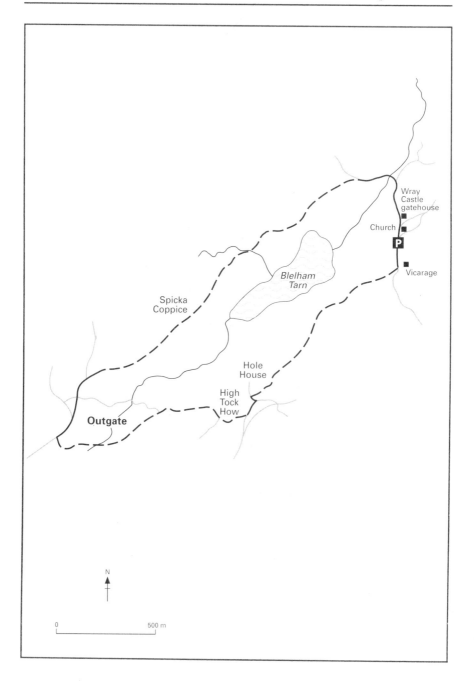

Wray
Castle
gatehouse

Church

Vicarage

P

*Blelham
Tarn*

Spicka
Coppice

Hole
House

High
Tock
How

Outgate

N

0   500 m

left again in just under 2 miles, heading for Wray Castle. There are good roadside spaces for several cars 100 yards or so beyond the castle gate-house.

Walk along the road towards Hawkshead for 200 yards, catching a glimpse of Windermere as Wray vicarage is passed. Leave the road by a footpath on the right, signposted to Outgate. Cross a meadow, with Blelham Tarn now in view, and reach a stone slab bridge over a stream and a kissing gate. On approaching an opening into a field, turn right following arrows on posts, cross two stiles and then rise fairly gently across yet another meadow. On the left is a tiny stream and coppiced woodland, rich in wild flowers. Behind, the long views include Ambleside, Wansfell Pike, and the Fairfield horseshoe of mountains.

Outgate Inn

On reaching the buildings of High Tock How, join the surfaced road, keeping straight ahead uphill, right in 100 yards along a farm access drive, and then left over a stile to follow a footpath to "Loanthwaite, Hawkshead, and Outgate". As the track divides keep straight ahead, downhill, for Outgate, turning sharp left as a barn is approached. Soon comes another junction by a prominent telegraph pole; either track leads to Outgate, but that to the right over a ladder stile dips and climbs steeply into the hamlet. More gentle is the left-hand route, reaching Outgate by the side of the inn after two sharp right turns.

With or without refreshment continue along the road towards Ambleside for a further 300 yards, turning right to follow a public bridleway by the "Outgate" boundary sign. After a short initial rise this apparently very old track descends steadily through and then along the edge of Spicka Coppice, with fine long views, Windermere again being visible. A section of open meadow reveals Blelham Tarn itself, the track here keeping close to the wall on the left. A beck is crossed at a ford, followed by a lightly wooded section and a kissing gate. From the far edge of the woodland the route lies straight ahead, aiming for a farm gate and joining the minor road. Turn right, uphill, to return to Wray Castle gate-house and the parking area.

Low Wray Church

9. Near Sawrey and Far Sawrey

Walk: Windermere lake and Sawrey Circular.

Length: 5^1/$_2$ miles

Rise and Fall: 320 feet. Easy gradients with one exception.

Underfoot: Generally good. One possibly wet section. 2^1/$_2$ miles of road – mostly very quiet.

Car Parking: Roadside space for 3 to 4 cars. Grid reference – 384952

Ordnance Survey: "English Lakes, South Eastern area" 1:25000.

Description

The country to the west of Windermere is quite different in character from the steep and craggy mountains of the Lakeland central core. The altogether gentler countryside results from the underlying geology; a variety of sedimentary rocks of the Silurian period have been moulded by the over-lying ice of the glacial period into a most attractive land-scape, well wooded and with plentiful lakes and tarns. This walk encompasses some of the best of this South Lakeland scenery, including a superb section of the Windermere shoreline. There is the added attraction of two of the best villages, Near and Far Sawrey, with the interest of Beatrix Potter's house at Hill Top, owned by the National Trust and open to the public in season. Also owned by the National Trust is the Tower Bank Arms in Near Sawrey; both villages also have other refreshment places, while Far Sawrey has a small general store.

The ferry between Bowness and the western shore at The Ferry House operates all the year round at 20 minute intervals, from early morning until 10 p.m. (high season) or 9 p.m. (low season), accommodating 18 average sized motor vehicles.

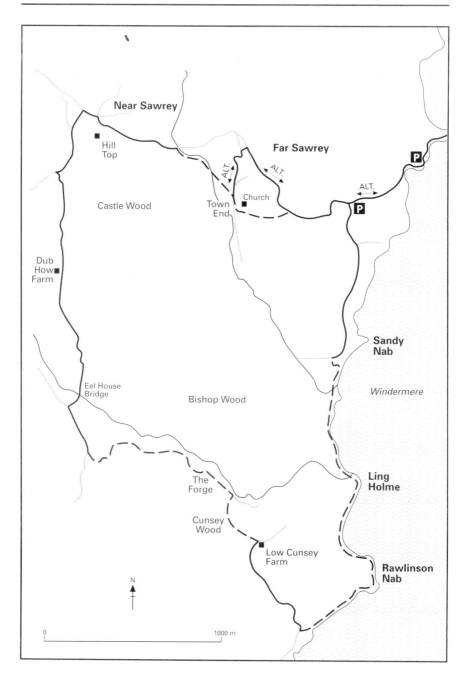

Route

To keep this walk as level as possible, the recommended place for car parking is at the junction of the Far Sawrey to the ferry road with the minor road signposted to Cunsey, less than half a mile from Far Sawrey village. There is an official car park closer to the ferry, but its use imposes an extra 70 feet of ascent.

Hill Top: Beatrix Potter's house

From the recommended starting point head for Cunsey along the minor road. From the official car park take the road towards Sawrey and shortly turn left-into a broad track running parallel with the lake shore, passing Ash Landing Nature Reserve of the Cumbria Wild Life Trust. The two routes come together in a quarter of a mile approx. and the minor road is followed for a further half a mile. As it turns away from the lake look out for a public footpath sign at a farm gate and stile, and turn left down to the lake shore. The path now clings most attractively to the shore, with little bridges, boat-houses and good cross lake views. The tiny island of Ling Holme is by the outfall of the Cunsey Beck, for many years the source of power for early industries including an early 18th century furnace and a bobbin mill, which were sited a short distance upstream. The woodland hereabouts still shows the evidence of centuries of coppicing the trees as a renewable source of timber for the production of charcoal and other purposes. Carry on to Rawlinson Nab, a fine promontory viewpoint and picnic place, with little south facing beaches, ideal for lake swimming.

The path leaves the lake shore in a further three quarters of a mile joining a quiet road by the side of a bank barn. Turn right and, at Low Cunsey Farm, turn left into a broad public bridleway rising and then falling gently through Cunsey Wood. On joining another track close to Cunsey Beck turn left. Very shortly the site of an early 17th century forge is passed; the present farm building was the office. The track continues past newly planted trees, eventually joining the Newby Bridge to Hawkshead road, one section often being wet underfoot. Turn right at the road and then right again in 300 yards to follow a minor road which crosses Cunsey Beck by Eel Bridge and then rises past Dub House Farm to Near Sawrey, turning right at the only junction on the way. As the crest of this road is reached, the views open up to the north, Esthwaite Water peeps through the trees and the Langdale Pikes are prominent.

Near Sawrey is a charming village, deservedly popular, and attracting large numbers of visitors to the Beatrix Potter house. Turn right at the main road; across the road junction by Buckle Yeat guest house, the house facing is the original "Ginger and Pickles" shop.

Follow the undulating road towards Far Sawrey; immediately after crossing a small stream take the footpath on the right, signposted to St Peter's church. Cross the stream on a footbridge and keep close to its side as far as a farm bridge; cross this and aim straight across the meadow to a small gate at the side of the end building of the Town End hamlet, almost directly in line with the church. Turn right on the road, pass the church, and turn left on to the "Ferry Hill" footpath. This path does rise quite steeply for a basically "level" walk, rather more than 90 feet in 200 yards or so, before rejoining the Hawkshead to the ferry road.

There is however an easier alternative. From Town End turn left into Far Sawrey village then right along the ferry road. The overall rise is very slightly less and is spread over a longer distance. Unfortunately the road can be quite busy, particularly when the ferry has just discharged a full load of vehicles.

Return to the parking place by a short downhill walk from Ferry Hill.

10. Loughrigg Tarn

Walk: Loughrigg Tarn circular.

Length: 1³/₄ miles.

Rise and Fall: Less than 100ft. No steep uphill gradients.

Underfoot: Good.

Car Parking: There are off the road spaces for several cars close to the road junction south of the tarn. Grid reference - 346040.

Ordnance Survey: "English Lakes, South Eastern area" 1:25000.

Description

Loughrigg Tarn is prettily situated beneath the steep slopes of Loughrigg Fell, in otherwise gentle countryside. The recommended circuit is a pleasant, undemanding stroll, although the return by Neaum Crag does involve some ascent, which can be avoided by continuing along the road from Loughrigg Fold. If desired, the walk can be shortened by using a footpath cutting across the north end of the tarn. A variety of refreshments is available at Oaks Farm.

Route

To reach the parking area take the Ambleside to Skelwith Bridge road, turning right towards Grasmere at Ellers Brow, just over 1 mile after Clappersgate. Set off on foot towards the row of cottages at Tarn Foot and then take the furthest left of three stony tracks - to "Loughrigg Tarn and Grasmere". The track keeps to the foot of the fell, with good views over the tarn and Neaum Crag opposite, and a rich variety of wild flowers

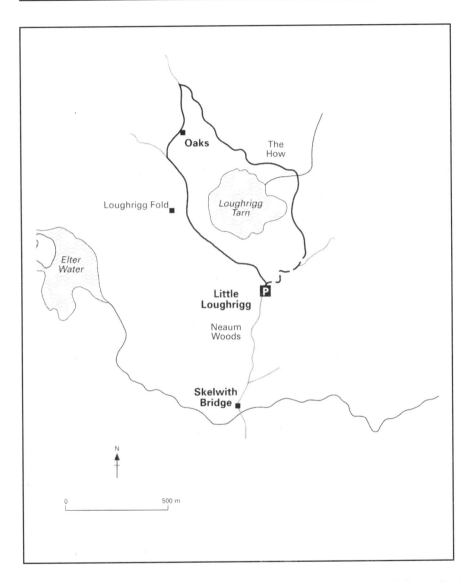

along the way. After a camping site is passed, a stile on the left marks the start of the short-cut footpath, which can also be used for tarn-side picnics. The Howe is soon reached, with a lovely cottage garden, probably seen at its best in the spring.

Continue until the public road is reached, turning sharp left towards Oaks Farm. At a road junction bear left and continue along the road to the parking area.

Loughrigg Tarn

11. Skelwith Bridge

Walk: Skelwith Bridge to Elterwater (with return options).

Length: $1^3/_4$ (one way) $4^1/_2$ miles (full circuit).

Rise and Fall: Nil (one way) 250 feet approx. (full circuit) with one steep section.

Underfoot: Generally good. The Elterwater track is often muddy in part, and the steep section of the return route is rough. Minor road for $1^1/_2$ miles.

Car Parking: Limited roadside parking in the vicinity of the Skelwith Bridge Hotel. Grid reference – 344035; alternatively, National Trust car park less than half a mile further along the Langdale road. Grid reference – 341037.

Ordnance Survey: "English Lakes, South Eastern area" 1:25000.

Description

The straightforward walk from Skelwith Bridge to Elterwater is one of the most genuinely level in all Lakeland. It is a great favourite, and deservedly so. In its short length it passes through a working slate dressing factory, close by a surging waterfall, through old woods and meadows, and close to an attractive and unspoilt lake. And all this with good mountain views along the way, dominated by the craggy mass of the Langdale Pikes ahead.

From Elterwater, four choices are offered. Firstly, to return by the same route; secondly, to use the Langdale valley bus (do check the timetable!); thirdly, to continue up the valley by the route set out in walk no. 12, thence returning by the bus. The fourth choice is to complete a good circular walk, but there is a fair amount of rise and fall, mostly at gentle gradients on the minor road or a good path, **but** at one point the path climbs 60 feet or so steeply up the bank of the Colwith Beck, on a rough surface.

Skelwith Force

Route

From Skelwith Bridge walk past the Kirkstone Gallery gift shop, noting the riverside picnic area and the choice of refreshment rooms for later indulgence, and carry on through the slate works. A well-used path is sandwiched between river and road, reaching Skelwith Force, a fine sight in spate, in 200 yards. Still visible are traces of the leat and conduit pipe which harnessed some of the power of the water for the works in earlier times. Continue to a gate and then across a broad meadow, keeping as far as possible to the path, which is low lying and usually muddy.

If the alternative start is made from the National Trust car park, cross the road and join the route in the meadow, saving the Kirkstone Gallery and the waterfall until the end of the circuit.

Anyone with an eye for geology will notice that the wooded knoll ahead is a "roche moutone" and that there are other glacial features in this area. Elterwater, a shallow, reed fringed lake, comes into view and the path traverses a lakeside wood, with many old trees showing evidence of coppicing. As the track leaves the wood to follow closely along the river bank, the village lies directly ahead, with the white painted Brittania Inn prominent. The village also has a post office/stores and public conveniences.

Unless, of course, refreshments are required at this early stage, for the return circuit turn left at the road, cross, Elterwater bridge, and carry on past the youth hostel, following the minor road for about $1^1/_2$ miles in total. At a junction, take "Colwith and Little Langdale", with a converted old bank barn on the right. The road is up and down, but at gentle gradients and the views are entirely pleasant. Ahead is Park Fell, with other named summits, such as Black Crag, while Loughrigg is across the valley to the left. As Colwith hamlet is reached, keep straight on for "Ambleside and Coniston" and cross Colwith bridge. looking carefully for the evidence that this was the boundary between Lancashire and Westmorland and wondering why sandstone was brought for quite some distance for the bridge construction. (In 40 yards a path on the right goes uphill for a quarter of a mile to Colwith Force, as a possible diversion.)

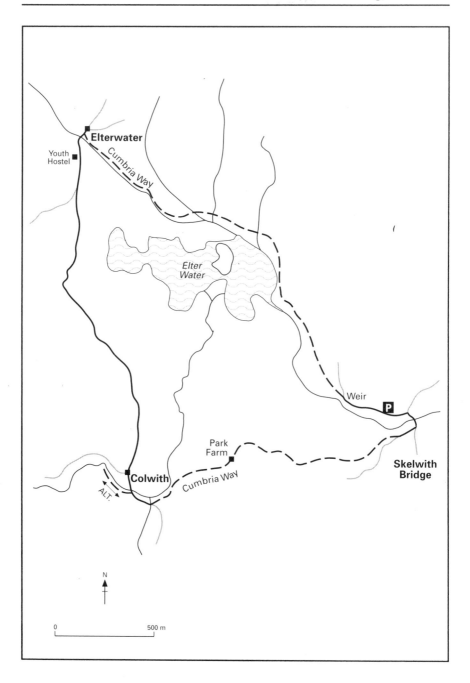

In another 100 yards along the road turn left at a stile, taking the 'Skelwith Bridge" footpath, part of the Cumbria Way. Now comes the awkward bit - a short, sharp ascent of the stream bank. The path then passes by the entrance to a house, at an iron gate followed by a stile, and rises a little further. On this open section the best views are, inevitably, behind; Lingmoor looks particularly impressive from this angle. Pass through Park Farm and descend steadily past another converted bank barn with attached cottages. Fork left by a big tree and continue through broad leafed woodland, forking right towards a wooden building and reaching the Skelwith Bridge to Coniston road. Turn left to return to the start. A left turn before joining the road leads to a new bridge, re-joining the outward route by crossing the river above Skelwith Force.

12. Langdale

Walk: Elterwater to New Dungeon Ghyll Hotel.

Length: $3^1/_4$ miles.

Rise and Fall: Modest at start. Thereafter negligible.

Underfoot: Very good but may be wet in part.

Car Parking: Car park in Elterwater village, opposite Brittania Inn. Grid reference – 328047.

Ordnance Survey: "English Lakes, South Western area" 1:25000.

Description

Langdale is one of Lakeland's most accessible and understandably popular valleys, easily reached from Ambleside. The scenery throughout is splendid, the gentle wooded country between Skelwith Bridge and Elterwater suddenly opening out to reveal the steep slopes and precipitous ˙cliffs of a ring of impressive mountains as Elterwater Common is reached. At the valley head the jagged outline of Crinkle Crags, and the shapely triangle of Bowfell dominate, while closer at hand are the Langdale Pikes, notably Pike O' Stickle and Harrison Stickle. The latter two have perhaps the most characteristic shapes in all Lakeland, quite unmistakeable when approaching the district along the main road from Kendal. A little behind and to the right of Harrison Stickle is the great cliff of Pavey Ark, sitting over Stickle Tarn, not visible from the valley bottom, but providing the water which cascades down Mill Ghyll in a series of rapids and small falls. The scenery of this upper part of the valley is greatly influenced by the ice covering which disappeared only a few thousand years ago.

Langdale is particularly well provided with long-established hostelries. At the start of the walk the Brittania in Elterwater has long been so popular that the tiny front bar holds only a small proportion of the customers and, even in bad weather, there is overflow to the outside accommodation. At the New Dungeon Ghyll, destination of the walk, the Stickle Barn has been provided to cater for casual refreshment, while three-quarters of a mile further up the valley the Old Dungeon Ghyll Hotel has long been the terminus of the infrequent bus service from Ambleside. Elterwater itself is a pleasant village with a post office/ general store, accommodation including a youth hostel, public conveniences, and a fine area of common land extending up the hillside towards Red Bank·

Langdale Pikes

Route

From the car park turn left along the road, cross the river and turn right
into the surfaced quarry access roadway. The road rises moderately
steeply, gaining 50-60 feet in less than a quarter of a mile. There is,
however, a turning space for cars at the top of this rise which could be
used to assist any member(s) of a group in starting what is otherwise a
very level walk. Car parking at this point is not possible. As the quarry
road bends to the left, take a footpath on the right, signposted on a large
rock, and descend to the river. Directly across is the sophisticated
Langdale time share development, on the site of the former Elterwater
gunpowder mills. The well-made track is part of the Cumbria Way,
passing between quarry spoil heaps and the river pool which provided
headwater for the gunpowder mills, to reach a footbridge by the Langdale Hotel, latterly Wainwright's Inn. Turn left on the valley road for 100
yards and then left again on to a signposted track at the entrance to
Chapel Stile village, rising for the first few yards. Turn left at a junction
and pass Thrang Farm. The rows of rather unsympathetic modern houses
along the side of the main road are very prominent here. Turn left yet
again to cross the river by a stone farm access bridge and follow the river
bank, past a farm camping site, with the main Langdale Pikes now in full
glorious view. Turn right to cross the river by a footbridge, again heading
towards the valley road and noting the slate field boundary stones, much
more characteristic of the Hawkshead area. Turn left at the road, and left
again in about 100 yards on to a public bridleway, a broad easy track
along the comparatively fertile valley bottom leading directly into the car
park opposite the New Dungeon Ghyll.

For the return to Elterwater the bus stops by the car park, but there are
alternatives. (For a slightly longer walk continue to the Old Dungeon
Ghyll, either along the road or, preferably, by a track which starts behind
the New Dungeon Ghyll and is best reached from the large car park on
the north side of the road. The extra distance is a little more than half a
mile. To return to Elterwater on foot, another portion of the Cumbria
Way may be used, but there is an ascent of about 170 feet. Walk up the
valley road for a little more than 100 yards and turn left on to the farm
roadway leading to Side House. Turn left at Side House and follow the
footpath steadily uphill round a shoulder of Lingmoor to reach Oak
Howe. Bear left to rejoin the outward route by the footbridge, and then
right to return to Elterwater. This return route has fine views across the
valley, but is rather messy underfoot).

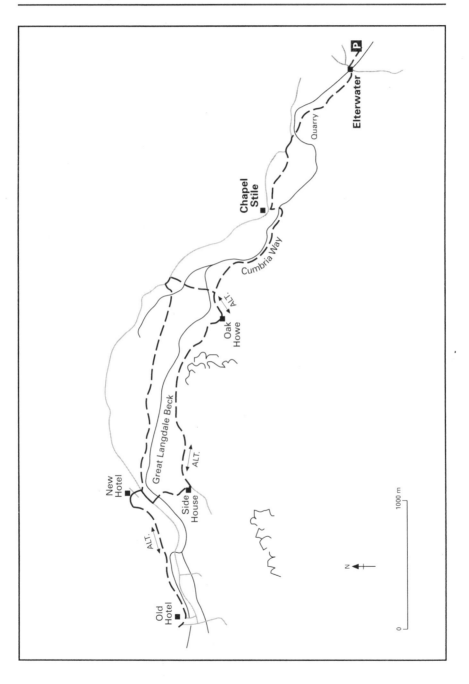

13. Little Langdale

Walk: Little Langdale circular.

Length: $3^1/_4$ miles, with shorter options.

Rise and Fall: Total ascent 360 feet, not continuous and no really steep gradients.

Underfoot: Very good.

Car Parking: Along roadside about 300 yards before the Three Shires Inn. Grid reference – 319032.

Ordnance Survey: "English Lakes, South Western (or South Eastern) area" 1:25000.

Description

Perhaps because it lacks the high drama of its greater neighbour, Little Langdale always seems to be a more relaxed, tranquil, valley, despite having the through road over the Wrynose Pass to the Duddon. That road is, in fact, narrow, often winding between walls, with blind corners, and is best avoided at Bank Holidays and other busy times. It is certainly not a road for anyone in a hurry.

Having said that, Little Langdale is otherwise quite delightful, the odd scars of disused quarries doing little to detract from the wonderful mixture of farmland, water, and mountain, with some woodland added in the lower part. To the south the dominant fell is Wetherlam, the north-eastern outpost of the Coniston group, whilst to the north the modest height of Lingmoor, with its final defiant upthrust of Side Pike, faces Pike O'Blisco across the Blea Tarn gap. In the adjacent valley of the Pierce How beck, enormous quarry spoil heaps dominate, apparently threatening to overwhelm the tiny hamlet of Hodge Close. On the other side of this valley, the working quarry at Moss Rigg is also prominent. However, these quarries are not by any means without interest. Just off the route of this walk, near Hodge Close, is a vast hole in the ground with a large pond in the bottom, claimed to be 150 feet deep, while close to Slaters Bridge is another hole, partially roofed over, and known locally as the "cathedral".

Slaters Bridge, one of Lakeland's finest and best known packhorse bridges, is actually a double bridge, one span being a well-made stone arch and the other a primitive clapper.

The Three Shires Inn, its name commemorating the coming together of the three former counties of Lancashire, Cumberland and Westmorland at the top of the nearby Wrynose Pass, has long provided accommodation and refreshment in Little Langdale.

Route

From the parking area walk up the valley road towards the Three Shires Inn for 100 yards approx. and turn left to take a footpath descending across a meadow to a footbridge over the R. Brathay. Rise across another meadow to an old lane leading to Stang End farmstead. Bear left past a galleried bank barn and then right, uphill, to follow a good wide track terracing above the valley of the Pierce How beck, with good views both to the mountains and, nearer at hand, to one of Lakeland's industrial landscapes. (A right turn at Stang End leads directly to the ford for a shorter walk).

At the top of a rise bear right at a gate and pass through an old broad-leafed wood before reaching Hodge Close hamlet, where old stone buildings are set among the quarry spoil, the extent of which shows clearly the scale of this former industry. At the far edge of the hamlet the route turns right, downhill, along a broad slaty track. (Before turning right, however, a 200 yard diversion may be made by going straight on , uphill, to the edge of the enormous hole mentioned above. Do be careful here as the edge is not fenced and the sides are all but vertical).

Back on course, take the middle track (at a triple fork), descending between stone walls, soon crossing Pierce How beck and rising to join a more major track. Turn right and follow this rough roadway to the ford and footbridge over the River Brathay.

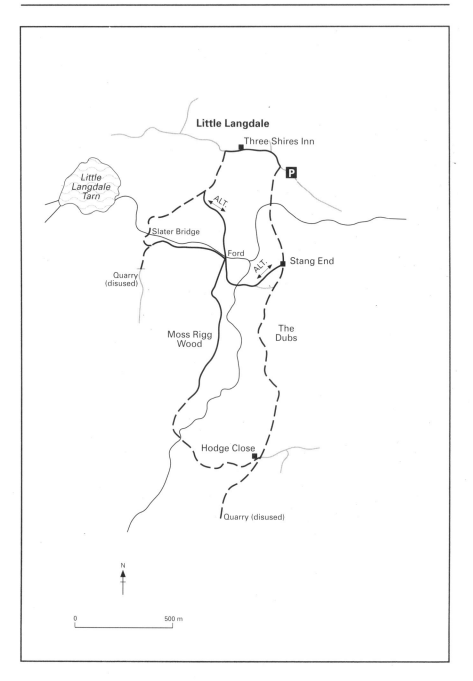

Quarry near Hodge Close

(Once again there is the opportunity for a shorter walk by crossing the river and taking the minor road opposite to its junction with the valley road, then turning right to return to the parking area)

For the full circuit turn left on the near side of the river. In less than a quarter of a mile, Slaters Bridge comes into view on the right, with a gate giving access to the bridge a little further. (Just before this gate, a rough track climbing to the left provides yet another short (but steep) diversion through disused quarry workings and ruined buildings to reach a large, partially roofed quarry hole, well worth seeing despite the disgusting litter in the bottom).

The path now crosses Slaters Bridge, turns right through a hole in the wall, and rises fairly steeply across grazing land to a kissing gate in a field corner. Bear a little right to reach a minor road down a flight of steps, turn left up the road and then right at the road junction to return to the parking area past the Three Shires Inn.

Slater's Bridge

14. Blea Tarn

Walk: Blea Tarn circular.

Length: $1^1/_2$ miles.

Rise and Fall: Very little.

Underfoot: Good. Almost 50% on surfaced road.

Car Parking: Small car park on far side of road, opposite Blea Tarn. Grid reference – 296043.

Ordnance Survey: "English Lakes, South Western area" 1:25000.

Description

The minor road connecting Great and Little Langdales climbs to a steep but not very high pass at the foot of Side Pike. Before the descent to Little Langdale commences in earnest, is a generally flat area with the little jewel of Blea Tarn at the foot of the steep slopes of Blake Rigg, rising to Pike O'Blisco behind. The circuit of the tarn makes a very easy and attractive ramble, a truly level walk among the mountains at an altitude of more than 650 feet.

Route

From the car park cross the road to the kissing gate and follow a broad, stony, track towards the near end of the tarn. To the right the Langdale Pikes are well framed between the shoulders of Kettle Crag and Side Pike. Pike of Stickle, Gimmer Crag, Loft Crag, Thorn Crag, and Harrison Stickle are all in view. Cross the outfall stream and turn right at once on to the lake shore path, which traverses an area colonized by rhododendrons, speculating as to who could have planted them, and why! The National Trust has recently commenced clearance work on these intruders.

(As an alternative route, the path which goes ahead, uphill, after the little bridge, can be followed; it bends right to rejoin the lower route at the far end of the woodland.)

The path emerges on to the open fell side, with the superb view now ahead, and is entirely straightforward in reaching the road at its highest point by a cattle grid. Turn right to return to the car park along the pleasantly undulating road.

Blea Tarn

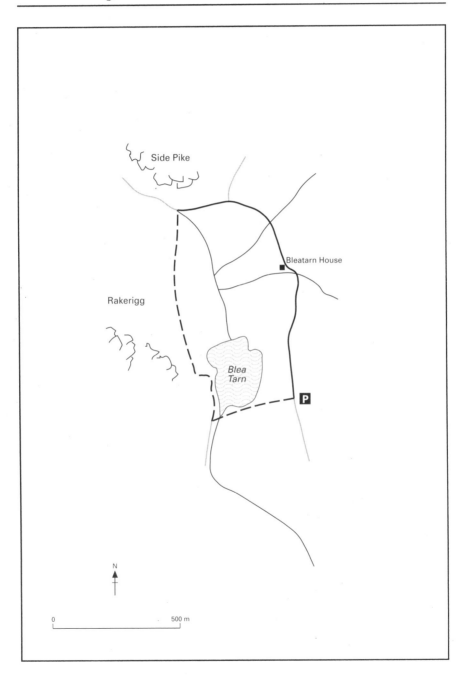

15. Tarn Hows

Walk: Tarn Hows circular.

Length: 2 miles.

Rise and Fall: 150 feet in total. No steep gradients.

Underfoot: Good.

Car Parking: National Trust Car Park (free to members) by the side of the Tarn Hows access road. Grid reference 325995. Special car park for the disabled, with its own level view point is a quarter of a mile before the main car park.

Ordnance Survey: "English Lakes, South Eastern area" 1:25000.

Description

Tarn Hows has been a favourite destination for generations of visitors to Lakeland. Strangely enough, older editions of Ordnance Survey maps did not use the name "Tarn Hows", but continued with the older name "The Tarns" long after the present name had become generally accepted. Accordingly, it took me 20 years or so to find my way to this delectable spot. So far as I was concerned if it wasn't named on the O.S. map it didn't exist! It is easy to appreciate why this is such a well-loved place, seeming as it does to encapsulate all the typical features of the more gentle Lakeland scenery, but with big mountains never far away. It may come' as a surprise to learn that the near landscape is very much man-made, the tarn being the result of damming a marshy valley to provide water power for a sawmill. The planting of a variety of trees – oak, rowan, pine, larch and spruce – has provided the perfect setting for this undoubted jewel.

Route

The only significant route finding needed is in driving to the car park.

From Ambleside take the Hawkshead road, being sure to turn left at Clappersgate. Three quarters of a mile before Hawkshead village, turn right by the old court house, soon reaching the hamlet of Hawkshead Hill. Turn right and then carry straight on at two further minor road junctions, now following signpostings to Tarn Hows. From the Coniston direction the minor road which appears to be the obvious left turn from the Hawkshead road is one way only – outbound from Tarn Hows – and it is necessary to continue further along the road towards Hawkshead before turning left and then left again to approach the tarn by its only access road.

Tarn Hows

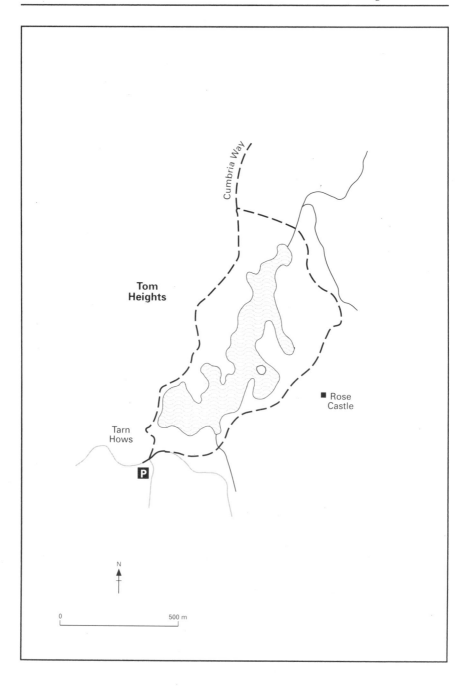

Tom
Heights

Cumbria Way

Rose
Castle

Tarn
Hows

P

N

0   500 m

From the car park it could not be more simple. Cross the road, noting the splendid mountain views which include the Langdale Pikes, Fairfield and High Street. Descend the grassy bank by a wide, well worn path, and follow this path in its circuit of the tarn, ignoring any connecting paths which lead away from the tarn.

16. Coniston

Walk: Coniston, Torver and lake shore

Length: 7 miles.

Rise and Fall: Approx. 400 feet ascent in total, well-spread. No prolonged steep sections.

Underfoot: Very varied. Mostly good, but some wet patches and broken ground. Three sections of road -about 400 yards in each case.

Car Parking: Lay-by on the Coniston-Broughton road at Haws Bank Grid reference – 299966.

Ordnance Survey: "English Lakes, South Western area" 1:25000.

Description

The Coniston area is very popular with holiday visitors and it may well be forgotten that the village was an industrial settlement, now a relic of long defunct mining and quarrying, served for 103 years by a branch line constructed by the Furness Railway in 1859. The lake is a fine stretch of water, made famous by the attempts on the world water speed record, successful and otherwise, by the Campbell family over a number of years, culminating in Donald's tragic death in 1967. The Coniston group of fells provides a superb backdrop to lake and village with the highest, that great favourite the Coniston Old Man, having a special place in the affection both of those who live there and those who enjoy mountain walking.

Obviously this walk avoids mountain ascents and its total of 400 feet is well spaced out and not really onerous; however, coupled with a distance of 7 miles and some roughish going underfoot, it does add up to one of the more strenuous circuits in the book. The rewards make the necessary effort very worthwhile. Lovely countryside between lake and mountain on the outward half, with the return along a delectable lake shore path make a winning combination. For a shorter walk there is an excellent short cut which reduces the distance to not much more than half of the full walk while still maintaining the essential character. The real loss is missing out Torver, where two inns compete in providing en route refreshments. Picnic opportunities by the side of the lake are abundant.

Coniston Water

Close to the start of the walk Coniston village has all the facilities expected of a busy holiday centre, plus a small museum, lake boating, and trips on the beautifully renovated steam yacht "Gondola". Across the lake, reached by a ferry in season, is John Ruskin's former house, Brantwood.

Route

Haws Bank is a hamlet close to a prominent church a long half mile south of Coniston village. A roadside layby provides space for 7 or 8 cars. Alternatively, the car park in the village may be used, but the amount of road walking is increased.

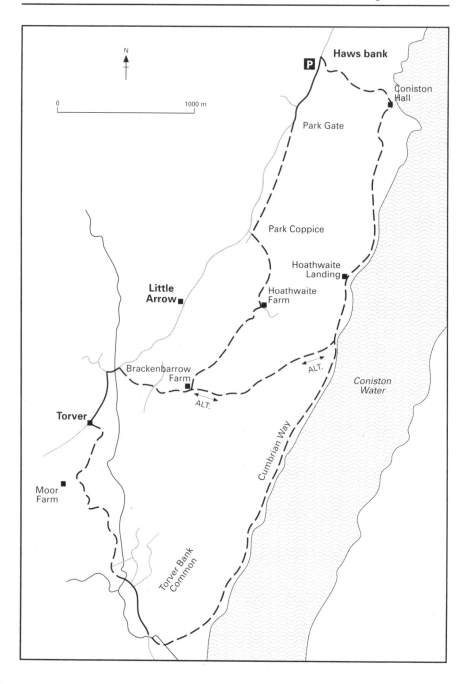

Set off uphill along the road, not pleasant at busy times; as the road bends to the right, go through a kissing gate straight ahead and follow a grassy track along the side of the trackbed of the much lamented former railway line, crossing a large meadow. At the far end the woodland of Park Coppice is entered, soon reaching the surfaced drive to a large caravan site, reasonably well concealed among the trees. Bear right along this drive, until it turns to the right to join the main road. Go straight ahead at the bend, still following the old railway line. At a stone wall, turn left through a farm gate and follow a not too distinct grassy path, bending left then right around a hummock. Aim for the dip in the ground ahead, bearing a little right towards a stream and a ladder stile. Ascend through the woodland, pass a mini waterfall, and emerge into more open country at a farm gate. Turn left along the field boundary towards Hoathwaite Farm. Turn right along the farm roadway and then left in a few yards to rise along a stone and grass track to a farm gate. Beyond, a grassy track continues to rise heading for a gate and stile on the edge of more woodland. The Coniston fells, seldom out of view on the outward walk, are impressive across a broad swathe of rich green farm land. Despite encroachment by bracken, the track rising through the woodland is well-defined, soon reaching an uncomfortably narrow stone stile. Cross a small meadow to a gap in the wall opposite, and continue along a slightly sunken lane between ancient hawthorns to Brackenbarrow Farm, highest point on the walk. Keep to the left of the farm.

(At the surfaced lane beyond the farm, a left turn reaches the shore of the lake in less than three quarters of a mile, by a good path descending through Torver Common Wood.) For the full walk turn right along a pleasant lane, go straight across a minor road, over a stile, pass a shallow, reedy, pond with adjacent muddy ground to another stile, cross the old railway line, and join the main road. Turn left towards Torver, which has two inviting inns, St. Luke's church, which has been visible ahead from Brackenbarrow Farm onwards, and a bus service back to Coniston which could be useful in bad weather.

Turn left in the village taking the Greenodd road and in less than 100 yards turn right into a surfaced bridleway by the side of a small caravan site. Shortly before Moor Farm turn left at a "bridleway to Sunny Bank" sign, soon reaching a gate and stile on the left, from which an embanked path leads downhill, to the side of a rushing stream and to Mill Bridge, with the former Mill house adjacent. Cross the bridge then turn left along a bridleway which rises to join the Torver to Greenodd road in 200 yards. Turn right to walk by the roadside downhill towards the lake. At a small parking area leave the road by an inviting track through the bracken, signposted "Coniston via lake shore". This is a delightful path, with extensive views over the lake. On reaching the shore it continues, rising and falling through the fringe woodland and latterly through Torver Common Wood for nearly two miles to Hoathwaite Landing. There are fine oaks, beeches, and birches along the way, with numerous shingly beaches offering alluring picnic and resting opportunities. At a division of tracks keep right towards a gate and then a post with yellow arrow.

From Hoathwaite, with its large-scale camping site, the route is entirely obvious as the track becomes broader and altogether more gentle, passing through the sites of historic iron-making "bloomeries" and another large camping site, with Coniston Old Hall, sitting under its massive chimney stacks ahead. Across the lake Brantwood stands out boldly from the heavily wooded slopes above the shore. At the Old Hall turn left uphill along the surfaced access road to return to Haws Bank and the parking place. For vehicles parked in Coniston village, go straight on from the Hall; a choice of routes ahead provides a return avoiding much of the road.

17. Duddon Valley

Walk: Middle Duddon circular.

Length: 5 miles.

Rise and Fall: Total ascent 600 feet, most of which occurs in 3 well séparated sections.

Underfoot: From the start to the stepping stones across the river is rough, stony, and muddy. Thereafter, a mixture of quiet road and reasonably good paths is much easier.

Car Parking: Forestry Commission car park/picnic area by the roadside three miles above Seathwaite. Grid reference – 236995.

Ordnance Survey: "English Lakes, South Western area" 1:25000.

Description

Even at times when Lakeland as a whole has large numbers of visitors, when Langdale and Borrowdale are overwhelmed, when the road tail-back into Ambleside starts at Rydal, the Duddon valley remains an oasis of tranquillity. The upper part of the valley is rugged and desolate, with the road over the Wrynose pass climbing high before its long descent into Little Langdale, but the middle Duddon is a rich mixture of bare rock, rushing waters, and dense forest. High above, the shapely peak of Harter Fell faces the less distinctive side of the Coniston fells across the valley. The Forestry Commission has planted huge areas of the flanks of Harter Fell, not quite with the sensitivity which would now be required, but the middle Duddon as a whole remains undeniably attractive. Farming has always been a hard business in such country, some of the broadest acres hereabouts being in the tributary valley of Tarn Beck.

Make no mistake about it; the walk described is no easy ramble. The riverside path is hard going; an ascent and descent with rocks, tree roots and, above all, mud; real clinging, boot-wrenching Lakeland mud, in profusion. The reward for making this effort is close intimacy with otherwise inaccessible beautiful green tumbling waters of the Duddon. For obvious reasons this path is to be taken slowly, preferably on a fine day. The remainder of the walk is quite different; across the farming country of the Tarn Beck valley, and back over Troutal Tongue which separates the two valleys. A little more than half a mile beyond the described route (and included in the suggested extension) is Seathwaite, a hamlet with the Newfield Inn and a church.

Middle Duddon from the car park

Route

From the car park cross the utilitarian bridge over the river and immediately turn left on to a vague, uninviting and muddy path which runs close to the boundary fence of the forest and, fortunately, does improve. Occasional wooden posts mark the way. Cross a tiny beck on stepping stones and bend left to pass what appears to be the remains of a large stone gate pillar, rising a little on firmer ground. In less than 50 yards turn left along a better path to Birks Bridge, spanning a fine rocky

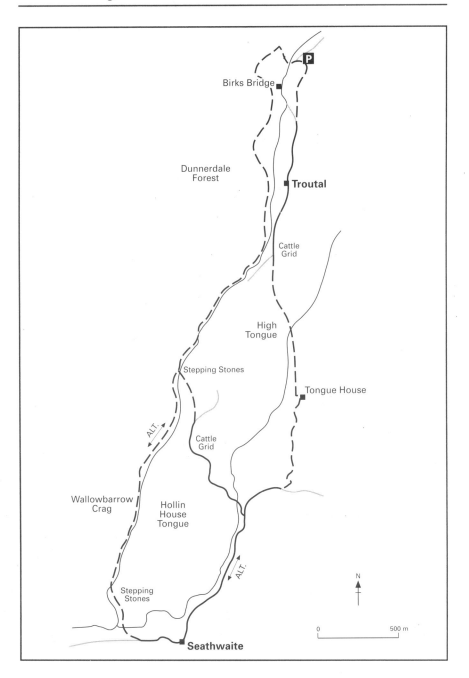

gorge. A rudimentary path continues close to the river for about 200 yards and then twists right and left, uphill, following white waymarkers, to a stile. Further ascent leads to an open viewpoint, with small rocky outcrops. At a junction, turn left to follow the signposted permissive path to Seathwaite, downhill over broken ground towards the river.

The path now clings close to the water most of the way to the stepping stones, passing a pretty little waterfall where Wet Gill descends abruptly through the trees. The stepping stones have a cable hand hold to facilitate the crossing but may be impassable if the river is high.

(For the extended walk, do not cross the river; continue along the permissive path for another mile of difficult footpath, including an ascent to the right to pass behind another knoll, to reach a choice of footbridge or stepping stones. Cross here and follow the footpath joining the road close to Seathwaite Church, crossing a bridge over Tarn Beck on the way. Turn left along the road to rejoin the route at the start of the Walna Scar road. The Newdield Inn is a short distance to the right.)

From the river take the footpath slanting uphill to the right, through the bracken, to the valley road. Turn right and follow the road downhill to the bridge across Tarn Beck. Beyond the bridge, turn sharp left into a surfaced road signposted to Coniston. This is the start of the well known Walna Scar road (unfit for motors) which crosses high over the Coniston Fells to the village of the same name. Turn left at the first junction, pass Hollin House, continuing along a lane towards Tongue House. This area provides some of the best farming country in the Duddon, contrasting remarkably with the earlier part of the walk. Fifty yards before Tongue House, turn left, cross a footbridge, pass Thrang Cottage, and follow a not very distinct track rising quite steeply to the left through the woodland. Emerge to the open top of Troutal Tongue, with exposed rocks, thick bracken, and good views. The track descends to a stile, with Harter Fell ahead, and continues to the valley road.

Turn right; along this section of road are thick lengths of wall which have become natural rock gardens. Troutal Farm is passed and, as the road bends to the left, take the signposted footpath through a farm gate straight ahead. The route is along the edge of some boggy ground. Head for the stile in the wall ahead. A good track traverses the pine plantation, emerging on the road close to the car park; turn left to return.

18. Middle Eskdale

Walk: Dalegarth and Boot.

Length: $3^1/_2$ miles.

Rise and Fall: Total ascent 130 feet. No steep gradients.

Underfoot: Generally good, but path from Boot to Christcliff has rough sections.

Car Parking: Large pay and display car park at Dalegarth station.

Ordnance Survey: "English Lakes, South Western area" 1:25000.

Description

Despite the absence of a lake, Eskdale is a popular valley, with a great deal of contrast throughout its length. The upper portion is as stark as anywhere in Lakeland, with the desolate marshy basin ringed by the majesty of Scafell, Scafell Pikes, Esk Pike, Bowfell, and the Crinkle Crags.

From the point where the Hardknott Pass descends abruptly to the valley, down to the King George IV Inn may be roughly described as "Middle Eskdale", with long established farms threaded along the valley bottom, the Woolpack Inn, the hamlet of Boot, and the upper terminus of the Ravenglass and Eskdale railway at Dalegarth, the railway being featured in walk no. 19. At Boot is a well-restored 16th century corn mill, open to visitors, a hotel/restaurant, and the Burnmoor Inn.

The present walk is basically a circuit of the low hump opposite Boot, providing a fair sample of the valley bottom countryside.

Route

The car park at Dalegarth station, complete with refreshments and public conveniences, is easily found. From the car park turn left along the road

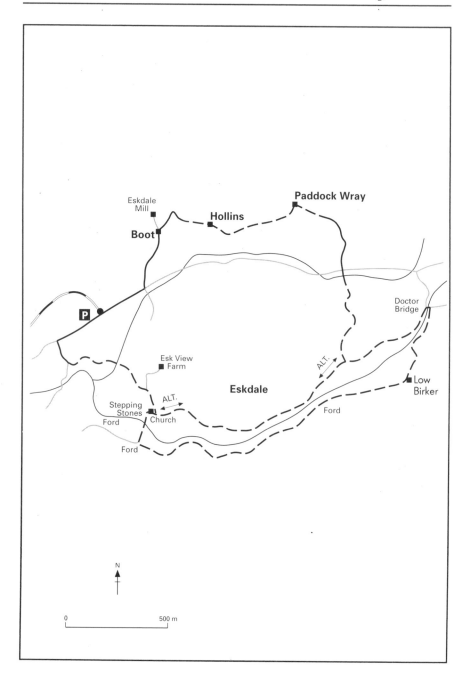

and left again at Brook House in 300 yards, towards Boot. The corn mill lies over the bridge, but our route is just before the bridge, a footpath to Eel Tarn. The uphill track follows the stream for 100 yards, at which point look carefully for a narrow stile on the right and take the grassy path, soon becoming stony, to Hollins Farm. At the far end of the farm take the footpath signposted to the Woolpack Inn. Several awkward stiles must be negotiated before turning left at a broad farm track, to Paddock Wray. Another Woolpack Inn footpath sign is at the far end of the farm; continue along the edge of the field, heading for a post which has a yellow arrow on its far side, and a stile behind. Head for the obvious gateway and turn right to reach the valley road.

'River Esk' at Dalegarth

Cross the road to the National Trust permissive footpath to Doctor Bridge. Helped by yellow arrows, the path is easy to follow over the rough pasture of Hodge How, skirting around a swampy area, and bending left to join a more important track. Across this section, the nicely pointed peak of Harter Fell has been the dominant landmark.

For Doctor Bridge turn left and follow the riverside path for half a mile. (To shorten the walk, turn right along the riverside path, to reach the church in about three-quarters of a of a mile).

Cross Doctor Bridge, a solid stone construction, and turn right immediately towards Low Birker, reached after a short, moderately steep ascent. Bear right here along a narrow lane and continue along a good, always obvious, track, partly in woodland and partly in the open, for one mile. Note the pinkish colour of the stones in the path, typical of the granite intrusions which have given us two "Red Pikes" in the western part of the district. At a junction take the public bridleway to the right, downhill, along the side of a tiny stream, to reach the river in 150 yards.

Cross the stepping stones, good family fun if the river is high, turning right then left to pass St. Catherine's church. Fork left into a bridleway in 100 yards to return to the valley road, opposite the Eskdale Centre. Turn right to regain the car park.

19. Lower Eskdale

Walk: Eskdale Green to Muncaster.

Length: 6¹/₄ miles.

Rise and Fall: Total ascent a little more than 500 feet, mostly occurring on the main road approaching Muncaster Castle and through the castle grounds.

Underfoot: Very good.

Car Parking: Eskdale Green railway station. Grid reference - 146998.

Ordnance Survey: "English Lakes, South Western area".1:25000.

Description

Lower Eskdale is dominated by the great mound of Muncaster Fell, not very high and not much more than half a mile in width, but more than 31/2 miles long, dividing the river from the Eskdale Green to Holmrook and Ravenglass road and from the Ravenglass and Eskdale railway line. Close to the head of this mound is Eskdale Green, most important village of the valley, with inns and two railway stations among its facilities. Ravenglass is situated between the western end of the fell and the sea, a port since Roman times, with the remains of Glannoventa fort to the south of the present village. The surviving stonework of the bath house is claimed to be the highest above ground genuine Roman structure in Britain. In Ravenglass itself, the only street leads attractively straight to the sea and the sandbanks; British Rail and Ravenglass and Eskdale stations are conveniently side by side. Nestling closer to the fell, Muncaster Castle, home of the Pennington family for 700 years and with close associations with King Henry VI, has a range of attractions on offer including tours of house and gardens and an owl sanctuary.

Refreshments are available. First stop from Ravenglass on the little railway is Muncaster Mill.

The Ravenglass and Eskdale Railway was originally of 3' gauge, constructed primarily to serve mines and quarries in the valley. As trade declined it became very run-down and in 1915 it was rebuilt to the present 15" gauge as a tourist line. With its superb rolling stock, well-kept stations, and the beauty of the area served, it provides the perfect return to Eskdale Green to finish this walk.

'Northern Rock' at Ravenglass

The lesser known countryside south of the fell, which is the true Esk valley is, by Lakeland standards, gently pastoral and most of this walk is easy rambling. The most strenuous section is the half mile of main road rising to the entrance to Muncaster Castle. Through the grounds of the castle the rise continues, but on a pleasant path.

Route

Leave Eskdale Green station by the approach road, turning sharp right into a public bridleway to Muncaster Head and Fell. Bear left as the

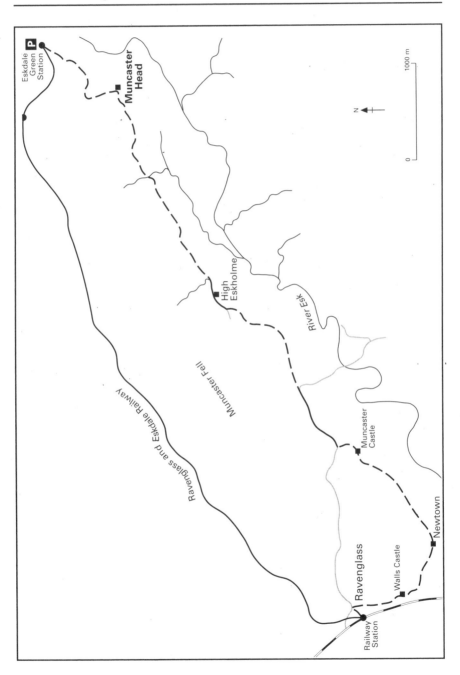

track approaches the railway line and carry on between mature trees to a small stream and stile. Go uphill through gorse to a large meadow where the path is ill-defined; keep towards the right-hand edge, making for a prominent tree-clad rocky knoll. Bend to the right after the knoll along the edge of another meadow, with Muncaster Head Farm below to the left. Join a major track at a signposted junction and turn left down to the farm, where old stone buildings are overwhelmed by basic modern farm structures.

Beyond the farm turn right and in 50 yards keep right again for Muncaster, rising slightly. The wide easy track now provides a good ramble for one and three-quarter miles along the foot of the fell, keeping just above the valley bottom with its broad pastures, lush by Lake District standards. Pass High Eskholme hamlet and follow the wooden direction boards to fork left across the private golf course and along the edge of the plantation opposite. At the far end of the plantation take a gate/stile on the left. The access road to Low Eskholme Farm is reached in 400 yards; turn right, cross over a surfaced drive, and rise to join the main road.

The first buildings of the Muncaster Castle complex are reached after a half mile uphill trudge along the road. Turn left at the "Muncaster Church, footpath to Ravenglass" sign, pass the squat church, the garden centre and cafeteria. On reaching the ticket kiosk, turn right for 40 yards and then left across the grass between the pond and the children's play area. Turn left at the track on the far side and then right, uphill, to follow "Ravenglass via Newtown"

The exit from the castle grounds is by a kissing gate and the contrast with the previous woodland could hardly be more dramatic; wide, open views of sea, sand, and Sellafield, over descending rough pasture. The track onwards is ill-defined. Keep just to the right of a knoll on the left, aiming for the middle of a conifer plantation, where a permissive path through the trees leads to Newtown farmstead. Turn right at the farm access drive, straight ahead at a junction, and join a surfaced road, turning right for Walls Castle which is the remaining portion of the Roman bath house. The road continues past a caravan site to the main road. Just short of the main road turn left through a small gate to take the footpath to the railway station for the return to Eskdale Green.

20. *Wasdale*

Walk: Wasdale Head.

Length: 3 miles.

Rise and Fall: 130 feet, at barely noticeable gradients.

Underfoot: Very good.

Car Parking: Car park off valley road, not well signposted. Grid reference – 182075.

Ordnance Survey: "English Lakes, South Western area" 1:25000.

Description

Wasdale is a mountain valley of great severity of character, with the steep slopes of the Screes plunging to form England's deepest lake, and the remarkable valley head comprising Kirkfell, Great Gable, Scafell Pikes, and Scafell. The similarity to many Norwegian fjords has been remarked upon.

The tiny settlement of Wasdale Head has been a farming community since at least Viking times and the over-thick field walls and great piles of stones bear witness to the efforts which have been required to provide a modicum of usable agricultural land. More recently, the Wasdale Head Hotel has good claim to have been the birthplace of British mountaineering, much frequented by the 19th century enthusiasts who pioneered the ascents of so many British and Alpine peaks.

This Wasdale Head walk is a gentle ramble at the feet of those mountains which have provided such a challenge to climbers over the years, a challenge not always successfully met as the graveyard of the nearby church shows. A strong candidate for the distinction of being the smallest parish church in the country, the building is almost hidden by one of the few plantations of trees in the valley. Behind the hotel is a lovely old packhorse bridge, reminding us that for centuries trade routes reached Wasdale via the high passes of Black Sail and Styhead.

Wasdale and Wasdale Head

For those who would prefer a longer walk in this superb valley, the circuit of the lake is an obvious choice, provided that patches of awkward scree can be negotiated without undue difficulty. Basic directions are included with this walk.

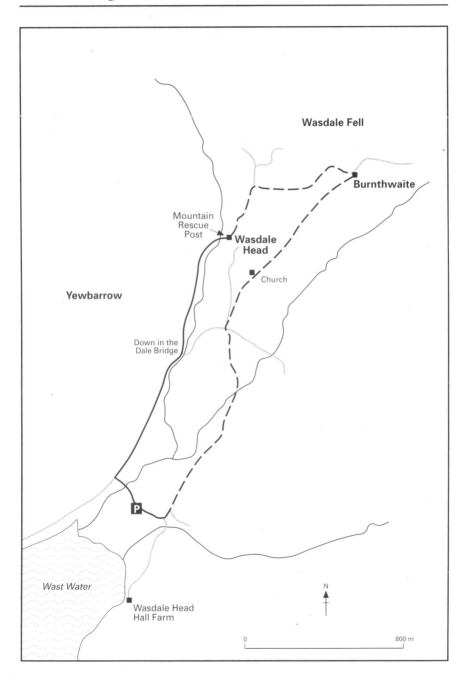

Wasdale Fell

Burnthwaite

Mountain
Rescue
Post

**Wasdale
Head**

■ Church

Yewbarrow

Down in the
Dale Bridge

P

Wast Water

■ Wasdale Head
Hall Farm

N

0   800 m

Route

The car park is found by turning right at the first opportunity after passing the lake, the lane being signposted to Scafell, Boot, and Wasdale Head Hall Farm. The car park is beyond the National Trust camping site.

Set off along the lane, turning left before the bridge over Lingmell Gill. Take the gate on the left into the camp-site and follow the camp roadway to the gate and stile at the far end. Great Gable is beautifully framed by Kirkfell and Lingmell ahead as the route crosses a stony flood-water bed, heading for a farm gate at the far side. Proceed through abundant gorse, cross a stream by stepping stones, and join the valley road at a stile/gate.

Head for the inn, but fork right at a car parking area, taking the public bridleway to the Styhead Pass. In less than a quarter of a mile the church is reached, the track continuing to Burnthwaite Farm. Most noticeable hereabouts are the thick walls and stone clearance piles. The path to the Styhead Pass rises clearly ahead but the farm is the limit for "level" walkers. Turn sharply left at the farm, following a path crossing and re-crossing a small beck. Join the major track from the Black Sail Pass and proceed to the packhorse bridge. After using any of the facilities at Wasdale Head, cross the bridge and turn left to follow a grassy track keeping close to Mosedale Beck before joining the road at a kissing gate by Down in the Dale Bridge. Turn right to return to the car park.

For a circuit of the lake the car park at Overbeck Bridge is a suitable place to commence. Walk along the road towards Wasdale Head, turn right to pass the camp-site and car park, cross the bridge over Lingmell Gill, and turn right along the access road towards Wasdale Head Hall Farm. After the farm, there is a path for most of the way but the odd patch of scree has to be negotiated. Whatever its disadvantages, at least this is one route where the walker is unlikely to lose the way! At the foot of the lake keep right, making for Lund Bridge. Cross the bridge and either head up to join the road or rake back along the side of the stream and then the lake shore, reaching the road more than half a mile further. The rest is obvious; should the road be quiet, the views ahead will more than compensate for the tarmac underfoot and the monotony of the route on the far side of the lake.

21. Loweswater

Walk: Loweswater circular.

Length: $3^1/4$ miles.

Rise and Fall: Total ascent 230 feet. The rise of 100 feet on the farm road to Hudson Place is the only climb of any consequence.

Underfoot: Good, but with some wet places. The roadside footpath on the return section is generally narrow and is rough underfoot. Approximately one mile is on a quiet public road.

Car Parking: Adequate roadside car park. Grid reference – 121224.

Ordnance Survey: "English Lakes, North Western area" 1:25000.

Description

Despite having provided the picture for the cover of the immediately post-war 1" Ordnance Survey map, treasured by the older generation of walkers, Loweswater remains one of the less well-known lakes, generally regarded as the poor relation of the Buttermere, Crummock, Loweswater trio. It is, nevertheless, a charming sheet of water with sharply contrasting vistas. To the north-west, above the head of the lake, is low hill country with a pronounced edge of the Lake District feel; to the south-east it shares the grand mountain panorama with its bigger neighbours, Buttermere and Crummock. From Loweswater, Melbreak is seen at its best; an impressive end-on view rather flattering this otherwise modest mountain. To the east the peaks of Whiteside and Grasmoor are dominant. The circuit is a well-varied mixture of typical Lakeland walking.

Route

From the car park walk north west towards Mockerkin. At the far end of a car pull-off (or parking) area with a telephone box, turn left at a public footpath sign, with stile and gate, and follow a grassy track heading

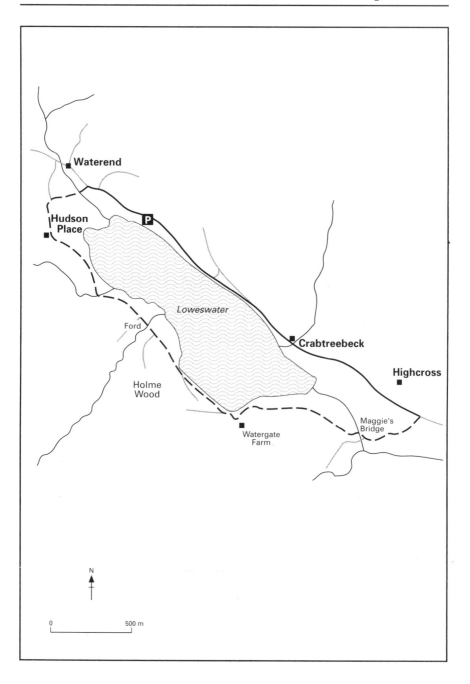

across the mire at the head of the lake. There are two further stiles and a wooden causeway which facilitates the crossing of the wettest ground. Join a surfaced road which rises quite steeply to the left before reaching "The Place" on the right.

Loweswater

Go straight ahead through a farm gate, passing the front of a house dated 1741. Signs point the way to the left, through another gate, now heading towards the lake on a good, descending, track. The great hump of Grasmoor is nicely in view before Holme Wood is entered. Soon there is a choice of track; either will do, as they come together again close to Holme Bothy at the far end of the wood.

The woodland is well varied, with some very old specimens of beech and other species close to the lake shore.

The National Trust-owned Watergate Farm is reached soon after leaving the wood. Turn left to follow the farm access road to a car parking area by Dub Beck and continue gently uphill to join the public road. Turn left to return to the car park. The road is usually quiet but, starting in 150m., beyond Crabtree Beck Farm, there is a narrow, stony, footpath which wriggles along for some distance between road and lake. At the far end of this path is a tiny shingle beach, very attractive for picnics. From this point the obligatory return to the road necessitates a steep little climb. Turn left to the car park.

22. Crummock

Walk: Crummock Circular.

Length: $2^1/_2$ miles.

Rise and Fall: Approx 170 feet in total. One moderate ascent from the lake accounts for half of this total.

Underfoot: Very good. Three quarters of a mile on minor public road.

Car Parking: Public car park in Lanthwaite Wood, by the side of the Lorton Vale to Loweswater road, just above Scalehill Bridge. Grid reference – 149215.

Ordnance Survey: "English Lakes, North Western area" 1:25000.

Description

Crummock is much the largest of the Buttermere, Crummock, Loweswater trio, a fine lake squeezed between the bulk of Grasmoor and Whiteless Pike to the east and the long ridge of Melbreak to the West. On a geological timescale, in the past Buttermere and Crummock were obviously one lake, with the present low-lying area of land close to Buttermere village resulting from progressive silting. Reputedly Lakeland's highest waterfall, Scale Force is hidden in a valley a little way above the south-west corner of the lake.

Mainly on footpaths, but with some unavoidable road walking, a circuit of Crummock may be made, but a fair amount of rise and fall is involved and the distance exceeds 8 miles. The present walk is a much less ambitious excursion but does offer, in miniature, a good mixture of woodland, open countryside and, best of all, what is probably the finest Crummock viewpoint.

At Loweswater hamlet, refreshments are available at the Kirkstile Inn from noon onwards, with a sequence of bar meals, afternoon tea, and varied evening catering. At the upper end of the lake Buttermere village has facilities which include two inns.

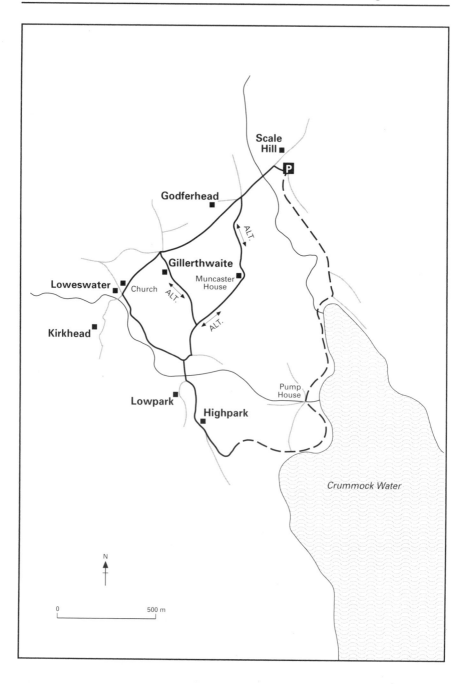

Route

The car park just within the edge of Lanthwaite Wood is visible from the road. Start along the broad, stony, roadway at the far end of the car park, with the infant R. Cocker close on the right. At a fork keep right, slightly downhill, reaching the shore of the lake at a shingly beach, a great spot for family picnics with long views up the lake. Turn right towards the weir at the lake outfall which has footbridges and a double "fish ladder". Continue along the shore, crossing Park Beck by another footbridge and passing the pump house, which is another reminder that, despite its natural appearance, Crummock is used for public water supplies. The knoll ahead is the promised viewpoint, setting the lake between good mountains on either side, with the ring around the head of Buttermere sealing off the head of the valley most effectively.

Near Crummock

Descend to a substantial stony beach and, immediately before the wall with the ladder stile, turn right, cross some muddy ground, head for a gap at the end of the wall, and then bear left uphill across a meadow. Head for another gap in a wall and follow the track descending gently towards High Park. Join a surfaced road as Low Park is approached, and cross Park Bridge.

A left turn at the next junction leads to Loweswater hamlet, with the Kirkstile Inn and a church. (Turning right and then left at the junction near Park Bridge allows a return either by Gillerthwaite or by Muncaster House, both routes being entirely straightforward).

From Loweswater hamlet the main circuit continues to the right, passing the church, to join the more important road, again turning right to return to the car park, crossing Scalehill Bridge on the way.

23. *Buttermere*

Walk: Buttermere circular.

Length: 4 miles.

Rise and fall: Very little. Total rise 100-150 feet. No steep gradients.

Underfoot: Mostly good. Can be wet in one or two places. Short section of exposed rock. Minor road for less than half a mile.

Car Parking: Two small car parks in Buttermere village. Grid reference – 174169.

Ordnance Survey: "English Lakes, North Western area" 1:25000.

Description

Reached by minor roads from Keswick or Cockermouth, Buttermere sits in a beautiful valley which it shares with Crummock Water. Formerly one large lake, extending further up what is now Warnscale Bottom, over a long period of time the silting effect of becks such as Sourmilk Ghyll has resulted in division into two lakes and a steadily shrinking Buttermere. Along the south-west side of the valley the mountain wall of Red Pike, High Stile and High Crag leads the eye round towards the dark crags of the lower Haystacks, favourite of the legendary Alfred Wainwright and resting place of his ashes. Fleetwith Pike, a finely shaped mountain viewed from Buttermere, stands guard over the valley head, forcing the narrow road to squeeze by its left flank, close under Honister Crag, on its long climb over to Borrowdale. Across the valley the slopes of Robinson and Hindscarth are less dramatic, but the great bulk of Grassmoor, sitting behind Whiteless Pike, is always impressive. Scale Force, Lakeland's highest waterfall, is tucked away out of sight above Crummock Water, but after heavy rain or with melting snow Sour Milk Ghyll makes a fine spectacle as it plunges over the lip from the Bleaberry Tarn corrie. Those with a geological interest will not be disappointed here; textbook corries, meeting places of the Skiddaw slate series with the Borrowdale volcanics, part of the pinkish coloured Ennerdale granophyre intrusion and other features are all around for the trained eye.

Buttermere village is very modest in size, but it does have two small hotels, youth hostel, camping site, and a tiny church of 1846 close by. Look for the shepherd and the sheep on the wrought iron gate by the porch. The lower car park, with public conveniences, is right by the side of the Fish Hotel, one of Lakeland's best known old inns and the home of the unfortunate Mary Robinson, the early 19th century "Maid of Buttermere", cruelly deceived by the "Hon. Augustus Hope" bigamist, swindler and forger, an early example of the complete con man, duly hanged at Carlisle in 1803. The story caught the melodramatic mood of the time, Wordsworth, Southey, and De Quincey all becoming involved. In more recent years Melvyn Bragg's novel of the same name fleshes out this now legendary story.

Buttermere church

Buttermere church

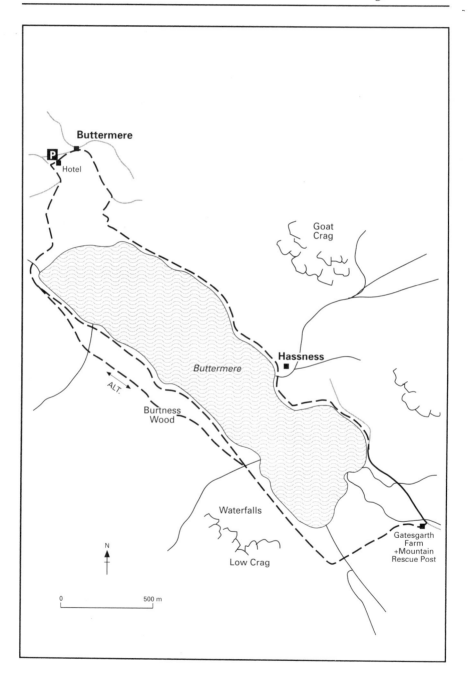

Route

From either car park start along the road towards the Honister Pass, taking the public bridleway through Syke and Willinsyke Farms and following a broad stony track descending gently towards the lake. There is a right turn and a short but comparatively steep section with rock underfoot before reaching the lake shore. The path continues through light woodland before reaching a very attractive section where it is squeezed between a steep rocky slope and the water, necessitating a tunnel through the rock. At any junction keep as close to the lake shore as possible. On reaching the Honister road, turn right towards the pass and carry on for about one third of a mile to Gatesgarth Farm, where there is privately owned car parking by the roadside. Prominent from the road is the white cross, low on the ridge of Fleetwith Pike ahead, "erected by friends of Fanny Mercer, accidentally killed 1887".

Immediately after crossing the bridge, turn right on to the public bridleway and follow the signs carefully through the farm, the destination being the lake shore. After negotiating a section which is often very wet, turn right by the far corner of the lake and follow the public bridleway to Buttermere. This is a straightforward route, largely through the National Trust owned Burtness Wood and with one section allowing a choice between true lake shore and a gently rising broader track further up the hillside. At the foot of the lake Sour Milk Ghyll is crossed by a small bridge, followed by a longer bridge over Buttermere Dubs, the lake outflow stream, and a broad easy track leads back to the village. Walking gently, with stops only to admire the scenery and to take photographs, the circuit will take about 2 hours. The lakeside picnic opportunities are virtually unlimited.

24. Newlands

Walk: Newlands Valley circular.

Length: 6 miles (3$^1/_4$ mile version available).

Rise and Fall: Nearly 500 feet but well spread and with easy gradients. More than half of the total ascent occurs in the first 1$^1/_4$ miles.

Underfoot: Very good. Some muddy ground just after Little Town.

Car Parking: Public car park off the Portinscale to Grange road. Grid reference – 247212. If full, there is a fair amount of roadside car parking close by.

Ordnance Survey: "English Lakes, North Western area" 1:25000.

Description

Despite its proximity to Keswick, the Vale of Newlands has always been regarded as one of Lakeland's quieter valleys, a good place to be when the honeypots are overwhelmed with human activity. Such comparative neglect is in no way indicative of any lack of beauty in the scenery. Indeed, shapely Cat Bells, the valley head of Dale Head,, Hindscarth and Robinson, and the grouping of the Causey Pike/Sail/Grizedale Pike fells form a superb mountain arena, while the valley itself has bright green meadows spread around centuries-old farming hamlets of weathered stone. The answer must lie in the lack of a lake or other focal point of particular interest.

The walk described keeps sufficiently far above the valley bottom to make the most of these views, Causey Pike and its neighbours being particularly impressive. The Newlands church, close to Little Town, is tiny, charming, and well-kept. Nearest refreshments are at the Swinside Inn, just over half a mile from the car park, with other inns and a post office/store at Portinscale.

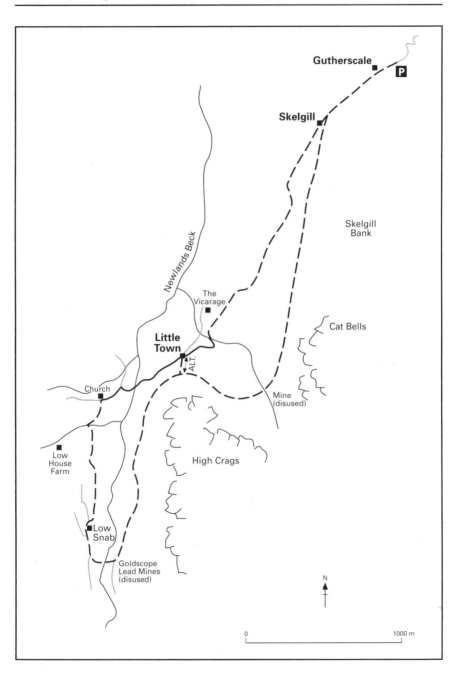

Gutherscale

P

Skelgill

Skelgill
Bank

Newlands Beck

The
Vicarage

Cat Bells

Little
Town

ALT.

Church

Mine
(disused)

Low
House
Farm

High Crags

Low
Snab

Goldscope
Lead Mines
(disused)

N

0   1000 m

Route

From Keswick take the main road towards Workington, join the A66, shortly turning left to Portinscale. Head for Grange and, where there is a sharp rise and left-hand bend keep straight on to a signposted car park. Walk on towards Skelgill, where in previous centuries three farmers shared the meagre acreage of usable agricultural land. Immediately before the farm gate, bear left along a pleasant track rising above the farmstead. This track, almost certainly an old mines road, keeps just above the farm intake wall, rising gradually to the highest point of the route. Ahead are the distinctive shapes of Hindscarth and Robinson; across the valley are Sail and Causey Pike, with Grizedale Pike peeping behind. Above the Newlands Pass, which carries a minor road to Buttermere, Red Pike is just visible. Mining spoil by Yewthwaite Ghyll reminds us that this peaceful valley was once a hive of industrial activity, lead being of particular importance, with the Ghyll now cutting deep through the old heaps.

The Vale of Newlands and Causey Pike

Cross the gill by the footbridge and continue to the right, soon going downhill. As the broad track doubles back to the farm at Little Town, keep straight on along a grassy track through the bracken, the church now being visible, sitting cosily amidst its sheltering trees. Join a wide, stony track continuing up the valley towards Dale Head, with Low Snab Farm opposite. As the spoil heaps of the former Goldscope lead mine are approached, turn right by the corner of a wall and cross the beck by a footbridge. Climb the opposite bank and turn right again towards the farm. Probably the best route through the farm is to fork left to pass above the buildings, then right through a gate to descend between buildings to the concreted farm road, turning left to head for the church, with the room which served as the valley school for 90 years attached at one end.

After the church turn right at the minor road, cross Chapel Bridge, pass a car park, and rise sharply to reach Little Town. Ahead is Skiddaw, 6 miles away, but with its impressive bulk rising high above the much nearer wooded hill at Swinside. At the far end of Little Town turn right at a lane signposted "Skelgill", bend left at a farm gate, cross Yewthwaite Gill by a footbridge and, as open farm land is reached, continue along a good footpath rising gently towards Skelgill. At the farm turn right and then left to return to the car park. (for a shorter walk, stay with the broad track as it doubles back at Little Town and then continue as above).

25. Borrowdale (1)

Walk: Rosthwaite and Seathwaite circular

Length: $5^1/_2$ – 6 miles.

Rise and Fall: 150 – 200 feet. No steep gradients.

Underfoot: Mixed. One short section on rock; otherwise generally good paths; $^1/_2$ or 1 mile on road.

Car Parking: National Trust car park, Rosthwaite (or Village Institute adjacent). Grid reference – 257149

Ordnance Survey: "English Lakes, North Western area" 1:25000.

Description

The upper reaches of Borrowdale approach the heart of central Lakeland; indeed, the valley gives its name to the hard, volcanic rocks which largely define the character of this glorious mountainous area. Above Seathwaite the main valley leads directly to Styhead, Great Gable and Scafell Pikes, while the tributary valley leads to Greenup Edge (for Grasmere), and the Langstrath (for Esk Hause, Bowfell, Stake Pass and Langdale). The valley itself has been scoured and shaped by the twin glaciers which met close by Rosthwaite and which have left such pronounced evidence of their activity.

Although most of the steep hillsides are bare and rock-strewn, there is enough woodland, including the ancient Johnny's Wood behind Longthwaite hamlet, to provide the contrasting scenery which is so typical of Borrowdale generally. Seathwaite, notorious for having the weather gauge consistently recording the highest rainfall in England, Thorneythwaite, and Yew Tree in Rosthwaite, are very old farmsteads. Also in Rosthwaite are an inn and a village stores. The route set out below is genuinely among the mountains without requiring any serious ascent.

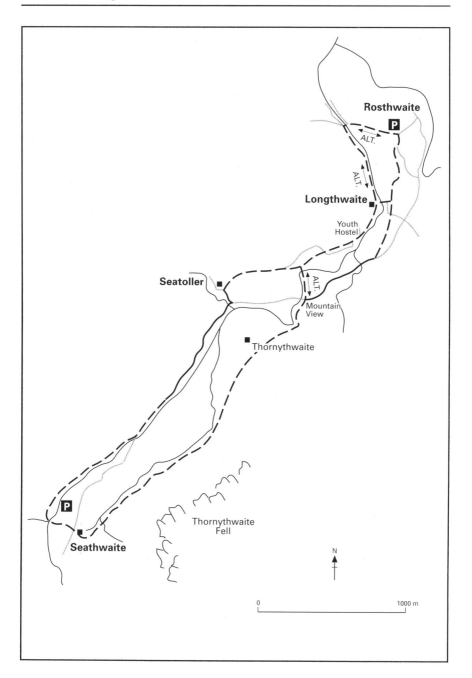

Rosthwaite

ALT.

ALT.

Longthwaite

Youth
Hostel

Seatoller

ALT.

Mountain
View

Thornythwaite

Thornythwaite
Fell

Seathwaite

N

0   1000 m

Route

Turn right from the car park and bear left at Yew Tree Farm, right again in 50 yards at "Stone Croft", and then immediately left at a gate, signposted to "Longthwaite Y.H.A.". A field path climbs over a large moraine and then cuts across the corner of a second field. Note the skill used in incorporating large glacial erratic boulders in the field boundary walls. At Longthwaite hamlet bear right on to an asphalted lane, cross the river by a stone bridge, and bear left through the gates to pass in front of the youth hostel. A riverside path now passes the cut end of a moraine, with 50 yards or so of exposed rock being a little tricky underfoot. The track rises along the bottom edge of Johnny's Wood, soon reaching a large holiday centre, where it rises again to a gate in the wall before descending to Seatoller. This tiny village has a restaurant, public conveniences, information centre, and is the terminus of the valley bus service. The valley road continues over the Honister Pass to Buttermere.

Turn left, down the road for a short distance, and then right, following the sign to "Seathwaite – 1 mile", which gives a distinctly optimistic estimate of the distance involved! After a long half mile, the road crosses the infant R. Derwent; here there is a choice-either to continue along the road to the farm, or to take the gate on the right and to follow a rather rough path close by the river, eventually reaching wooden bridges over Sour Milk Ghyll and the river before turning left to reach the farm. Either way, the Ghyll makes a fine sight during or after heavy rain, as it cascades down from its hanging valley under the cliffs of Brandreth. The view ahead is dominated by the great mountains, with Glaramara high on the left. Before reaching the bridge over Sour Milk Gill, look out for a memorial tablet to John Bankes Esq. a replacement for one destroyed by Victorian vandals in November 1887.

At Seathwaite, turn right and then left to follow a "public footpath" sign, through a gate, and across a field with four stone cairns, to another gate. The track continues towards Thorneythwaite Farm, along the foot of a hillside liberally strewn with glacially deposited boulders. Just before the farm, turn right immediately before a gate and continue, to join the farm access road; on the left the great thickness of the wall shows the extent of the stone clearance which was required before the adjacent field could be cultivated. The farm road follows the river to the main valley road, opposite the "Mountain View" houses. Here there is yet another choice – a) to cross the road and then the river by a stone bridge, turn right and retrace the outward route past the Youth Hostel to the bridge at Longthwaite hamlet. Do not cross, but carry on along the permissive path towards Keswick, shortly passing a cottage which has a line drawn across its front door, marking the high water level of the 1966 floods. The path clings to the river bank as far as an old ford with stepping stones Cross the river and return to Rosthwaite. Should the river be in spate, or the balance in doubt, continue for a further 300 yards to a bridge and return along the far side of the river.

Option b) is to turn right along the valley road for less than half a mile, climb a stile over the wall on the left at a "Rosthwaite" sign, cross the field to a ladder stile, and proceed along the crest of a splendid moraine to Longthwaite, thence retracing the outward route to Rosthwaite.

Farm buildings, Rosthwaite

26. Borrowdale (2)

Walk: Grange to Rosthwaite.

Length: $2^1/_2$ miles.

Rise and Fall: Total ascent 100 feet approx. No severe gradients.

Underfoot: Generally good. A small amount of rough, stony, ground.

Car Parking: By the river at Grange in Borrowdale. Grid reference – 253175.

Ordnance Survey: "English Lakes, North Western area" 1:25000.

Description

This is one of several fine short walks in this most lovely of Lakeland valleys, passing through what is arguably the most interesting part of the whole valley – the "jaws" of Borrowdale – where the steep slopes of Castle Crag and, of Kings How opposite squeeze river and road tightly together among the superb woodland. The valley sides are scarred by old quarry workings, generally well hidden by the trees, but those beside the track are worth seeking out.

Both Grange, with its double bridge over the R. Derwent and Rosthwaite with its Rogue Herries literary connections, are attractive small villages with refreshments available at each end of the walk. The use of the valley bus service is recommended for the return, but it would be no hardship to retrace the route on foot or to walk back along the road.

Route

There is parking space for about eight cars by the end of the double bridge at Grange, where there is a superb picnic spot by the side of the river. Walk into the village, pass the cafe, and turn left immediately to follow a public bridleway signposted to Rosthwaite. A short distance along the bridleway is another small car parking area. Shortly after

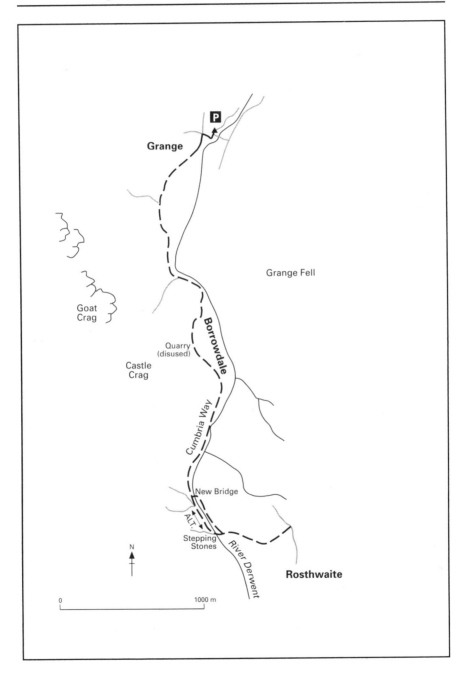

passing the National Trust Hollows Farm sign, turn left, following a gently rising broad stony track, again keeping left towards the river after passing a camping site. At a "footpath to Rosthwaite" sign, keep left, soon reaching a stony section which climbs fairly steeply before turning left yet again at a gap in the wall. Continue through the woodland. turning sharp left just over the crest of the rise to head downhill towards a stone cairn.

At a quarry spoil heap on the right, a short sharp pull uphill leads to a rock face with interesting mineral colouration and a large rock arch, almost forming a cave. The latter can be seen without the sharp ascent by continuing a little further along the main path before diverting to the right. The attractive and varied woodland which is such a feature of this walk is looked after by the National Trust. The R. Derwent is crossed by a substantial stone bridge; those with more sporting instincts can continue for a further 300 yards up river to cross by stepping stones, more fun when the water is high. Either way, a lane now leads straight to Rosthwaite, with post office/ stores, hotel, public conveniences, and a not very frequent bus service back to Grange.

River Derwent and bridge near Rosthwaite

27. Derwentwater - West Shore

Walk: Nichol End to Brandelhow Bay.

Length: 2¹/₂ miles.

Rise and Fall: Less than 50 feet in total. No steep gradients.

Underfoot: Very good. A small amount of wet ground.

Car Parking: It is recommended to use the large pay and display car park close to the Theatre by the Lake in Keswick, with a short trip on the Ferry to Nicol End.

Ordnance Survey: "English Lakes, North Western area" 1:25000.

Description

Within easy striking distance of Keswick, this short lakeside ramble encompasses most of the ingredients which make Lakeland walking so fascinating; views of lake and mountains, fine mixed woodland, and a good level path underfoot. There is scope for extending, diminishing, or otherwise varying the walk, and a few suggestions are made at the end of the basic route. A ferry service using traditional old launches circles the lake in both clockwise and anti-clockwise directions, calling at seven jetties at approx. hourly intervals in high season, less frequently in low season, and not at all in winter. A return by this service is much the most enjoyable way to end this walk. Derwentwater must rank among the prettiest of the lakes, with its four sizeable wooded islands and the bulk of Skiddaw towering over Keswick ahead.

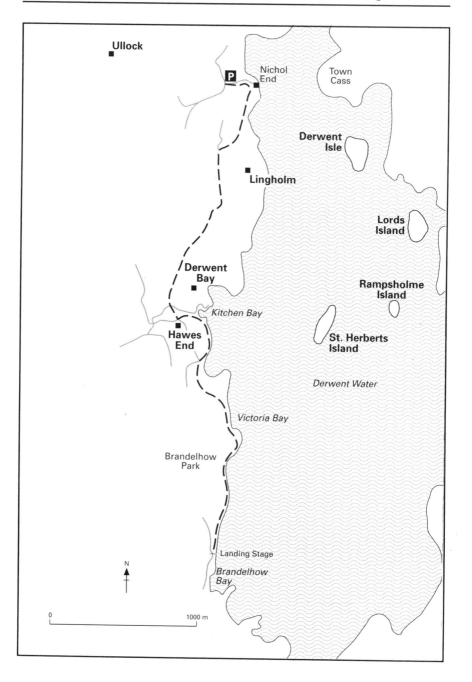

Ullock

Nichol End

Town Cass

Derwent Isle

Lingholm

Lords Island

Derwent Bay

Rampsholme Island

Kitchen Bay

Hawes End

St. Herberts Island

Derwent Water

Victoria Bay

Brandelhow Park

N

Landing Stage

Brandelhow Bay

0   1000 m

Route

To reach the recommended car parking, take the main A66 Workington road from Keswick, turning left for Portinscale and Grange in 1¹/₂ miles. After weaving through Portinscale village, in half a mile turn left into a roadway leading to Nichol End marina, by the entrance to Fawe Park. The roadway is double tracked for a few yards and there is space for six or seven vehicles.

Derwentwater

Walk down to the lake shore at the marina and turn right behind the marina building to climb briefly but fairly steeply up a broad track. Pass straight across the surfaced drive leading to Fawe Park and continue along the same track, passing behind the house. The entrance to Lingholm gardens is soon reached. Take the little gate on the right, following the "public footpath to Cat Bells". The woodland hereabouts is rich and diverse with thickets of young saplings competing to break through into the forest canopy above. A welcome treat is a sudden view of the shapely cone of Cat Bells, directly ahead. A kissing gate leads to an open meadow, with the track causewayed across some wet ground. At the far side is another gate, a stream, and a short rise into more woodland, now primarily coniferous. Walla Crag comes into view, left, above the as yet invisible lake, before a surfaced road is reached at a kissing gate.

Turn left on the road and in less than 50 yards left again by a redundant old iron kissing gate, to descend quite steeply to the lake shore, where a shingly beach edges the tiny Kitchen Bay, with its ferry jetty. Bear right to follow close to the lake shore, soon passing another jetty. The nearest island is St. Herbert's, legendary home of the eponymous saint, and the lake shore itself is attractively fringed with mature beeches and oaks. Kings How shows up well above the Borrowdale valley side as the jetty just to the north of Brandlehow Bay is approached and the walk is over all too soon.

The clockwise ferry provides the shorter and cheaper return to Nichol End. However, the walk can be extended for a further 2 miles, as the path carries on through Manesty Park before turning sharp left to cross the marshy ground at the head of the lake, with a footbridge over the R Derwent, to reach the Borrowdale valley road a little way above the Lodore Hotel. Turn left, and then left again by the hotel towards the landing stage. The walk may, of course, be shortened by returning from either of the intermediate landing stages.

28. Keswick

Walk: Derwentwater east side, including Friar's Crag.

Length: $2^1/_4$ miles (extendible).

Rise and Fall: Negligible.

Underfoot: Good, but one section of rough, stony, ground along the lake shore.

Car Parking: Pay and display public car park close to Keswick boat landings. Grid reference – 266229

Ordnance Survey: "English Lakes, North Western area" 1:25000.

Description

Derwentwater is a beautiful lake, perhaps seen at its best when an early morning haze softens the outline of the surrounding fells but does nothing to spoil their reflections in the tranquil water on a windless day. Ever since John Ruskin's advocacy, Friar's Crag has been celebrated as the classic viewpoint; it is certainly good, but along the length of this walk other opportunities occur, either to set the lake against the abrupt hillsides of the Borrowdale fells to the south, or to gaze north, where the perfect proportions of Skiddaw rise high above Keswick.

Another attraction is the wooded islands, three of the four having historical interest; Derwent Isle, close to Friar's Crag, was the home of the German miners recruited in the 16th century to exploit the mineral resources of the area; St Herbert' s Island was reputedly the home of the saint of the same name, becoming a place of pilgrimage; Lord's Isle has the site of the house of the Earls of Derwentwater.

As mentioned in walk no. 27, traditional launches operate a scheduled service, calling at seven jetties (including Keswick landings) around the lake, highly recommended for the return to Keswick, with the Borrowdale bus as an alternative. One advantage of starting a walk so close to

Keswick is that no motor car is required; from the town centre to the boat landings is less than half a mile.

Derwentwater

Route

The boat landings and the adjacent large car park are well signposted off the Borrowdale road to the south of the town centre. From the car park turn left, passing the theatre and the public conveniences on the way to the lake. Continue along the shore, passing a memorial tablet to Canon Rawnsley, founder of the National Trust, so important to the maintenance and the well-being of Lakeland. Derwent Isle is close on the right, and the celebrated viewpoint is very soon reached.

A short back track is necessary before bearing right down a flight of easy pitched stone steps and following the lake shore around Strandshag Bay. The track continues along the edge of marshy woodland, over a footbridge, and through a gate at the far end of the wood. Turn right here,

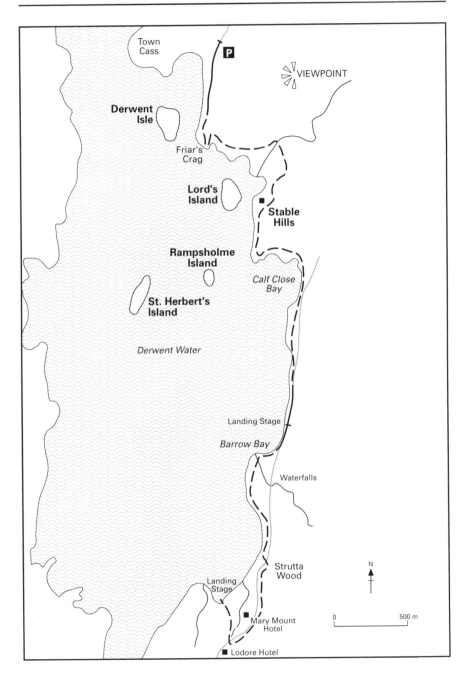

Town
Cass

VIEWPOINT

**Derwent
Isle**

Friar's
Crag

**Lord's
Island**

■ **Stable
Hills**

**Rampsholme
Island**

*Calf Close
Bay*

**St. Herbert's
Island**

Derwent Water

Landing Stage

Barrow Bay

Waterfalls

Strutta
Wood

Landing
Stage

N

■ Mary Mount
Hotel

0   500 m

■ Lodore Hotel

passing Stable Hills and Lord's Island, heading for Calf Close Bay. Rampsholme Island is close, St. Herbert's Island more distant, with the summit of Cat Bells-rising steeply behind. The track and the Borrowdale road are now closely together, with some up and down which can be avoided by walking on the rough stones of the lake shore. It soon becomes essential to keep even closer to the lake, as the path becomes tightly squeezed between rock faces and the water.

Ashness Gate jetty follows this section, with the launches offering a choice of a short ride directly back to Keswick or a longer and more circuitous trip around the lake.

(To extend the walk, continue along the shore of Barrow Bay, crossing Barrow Beck by a footbridge, the Lodore Swiss Hotel standing out well against the wooded hillside, as the path reaches Kettlewell car park. Cross the road and take the broad track opposite, through Strutta Wood, which avoids half a mile of road but does go up and down somewhat over roughish ground. On regaining the road, to return by launch cross over to a roadway leading directly to the Lodore jetty. The alternative is to wait for the bus by the hotel. The famous Lodore Falls are behind the hotel, the track starting just beyond the main building, but there is quite a climb through the woodland.

It will be obvious that if sufficient time and energy remain, the walk can be further extended around the lake, by turning right just past the hotel and following the track across the swampy ground to a prominent footbridge and then to the Manesty shore and High Brandlehow landing stage (or even beyond, following walk no. 27 in reverse!).

29. Threlkeld

Walk: Threlkeld circular.

Length: 3 miles.

Rise and fall: 250 feet.No steep gradients.

Underfoot: Very good One wet meadow.

Car Parking: Small car park in Threlkeld. Grid reference – 318256.

Ordnance Survey: "English Lakes, North Western area" 1:25000.

Description

Threlkeld is a pleasantly unassuming village situated 4 miles east of Keswick and now, happily, by-passed by the main A66 Keswick to Penrith road. The winding main street has a post office/general store and two inns, one of them dating from the 17th century.

However, the great glory of Threlkeld is its setting close to the foot of mighty Blencathra (also known as Saddleback), the arms of the south ridges – Gategill Fell, Hall's Fell, and Doddick Fell – reaching out almost to embrace the village. To the south and to the west are longer views; Clough Head at the northern end of the bulky ridge of Helvellyn, the Vale of St. John and, more distant, the shapely grouping of Cat Bells and the north western fells around Grisedale Pike.

The outward half of this walk is across a succession of upland meadows following a lightly used path, with the views paramount. The return is along the trackbed of the disused Keswick to Penrith railway line, with the R. Greta weaving to and fro in close company. Woodland, bridges and a short tunnel add interest to this part of the walk. Walkers with an interest in railways will know that the Cockermouth, Keswick and Penrith Railway was opened to goods traffic in 1864 and to passengers early in 1865. The engineer was Thomas Bouch, whose claim to fame rests with his unfortunate Tay Bridge, which collapsed during a storm in

December, 1879, with the loss of a train and many lives. At Cockermouth there was a connection with the Cockermouth and Workington Railway, and the main target of the promoters of the railway was the traffic in iron ore from West Cumberland to the foundries of the north-east, with a return traffic in coke to the ironworks around Workington. Construction of the 31 miles of line necessitated no less than 135 bridges, 8 of them over the 7 mile length of the River Greta.

Unfortunately but inevitably, traffic, including the once busy passenger service, declined steadily, particularly after World War II, and Keswick to Penrith closed in 1972, the section to the west of Keswick having closed a few years previously.

Threlkeld: disused railway line

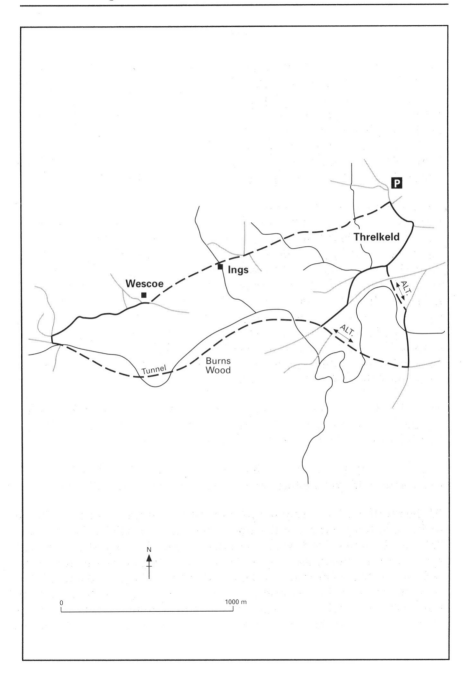

Route

The car park in Threlkeld is beside the minor road serving the Blencathra Centre, to the north of the village street and about 300 yards from that street. From the car park walk towards the village centre for 100 yards and turn right at a public footpath sign for Wescoe and Keswick, pass through a kissing gate and keep a more or less straight line across several meadows. The path is not always well-defined underfoot, but the fields are small and there is always a gate or stile in view at the far which gives the line, many being marked with arrows on posts.

To the right Blencathra dominates, while ahead the long views over Keswick to Grisedale Pike and its neighbours are superb. The house named Ings is passed and the path continues on the same line, traversing a rather boggy meadow before reaching the farming hamlet of Wescoe. Go straight ahead to follow a surfaced lane downhill beside a normally tiny beck whose banks show clearly the erosion power of Lakeland streams in spate. At the bottom of the hill a wider stream is crossed; turn left at once through a gate marked "Keswick railway footpath and stone circle", cross a plank bridge and reach the disused railway line. To the right is a former lineside building renovated by the National Park Authority to provide shelter and useful information concerning the line and its environment.

The route is to the left, crossing the Greta for the first time by bridge, typical of this line. The track-bed rises very gently through woodland keeping close to the river in its attractively wooded valley.

The river is crossed a second time, followed by a 30 yard tunnel under a rocky spur, with yet another river crossing immediately following.

At the fourth river crossing the path leaves the railway, rising to join the main road. Keep left along the side of the road for 200 yards then turn left into the minor road which becomes Threlkeld village street and left again at Blease Road, leading to Blencathra, to regain the car park. (The walk along the main road can be avoided by making a detour; do not cross the river at the last bridge, but carry on along a footpath on the right under the main road, rejoining the railway until it reaches the road along St John's in the Vale. Turn left, cross the River Glenderamackin and then left again on the field path which goes straight across the main road to join the village street).

Virtually all the ascent in this walk comes at the end with the rise to the main road and then a steady pull up through the village. Perhaps a quarter of this ascent could be avoided by finding a discreet parking place in the main part of the village.

30. St. John's in The Vale

Walk: St. John's in the Vale and Naddle Valley circular.

Length: 6 miles.

Rise and Fall: Total ascent; 400 - 500 feet. Some moderately steep gradients.

Underfoot: Very mixed. Rough narrow paths and broad, easy, lanes.

Car Parking: Car park/picnic area at Legburthwaite. Grid reference - 318195

Ordnance Survey: "English Lakes, North Western area" 1:25000.

Description

Arguably, this walk should not really be included in a "level" walks book. The total rise and fall of the preferred route is quite considerable, occurring principally in the crossing of the mini pass between High Rigg and Low Rigg summits, at the crest of which are found St. John's in the Vale church and the Carlisle Diocesan Youth Centre. However, at least some of the total ascent can be avoided in the early stages by keeping to the valley bottom (see "route" below). Ironically, this overall reduction in ascent is achieved at the expense of having a continuous climb of nearly 300 feet from Bridge House to the church, some of it at quite steep gradients.

Having given an appropriate apology (and a health warning !), I have to say that the attractions of the Vale of St. John, highly regarded as a "romantic" valley in Victorian times, are worth making an extra effort.

Mighty Blencathra (also known as Saddleback) is beautifully framed between the steep valley sides; old farmsteads compete for the all too few bright green valley bottom fields, through which the St. John's Beck meanders, carrying whatever water Manchester can spare from Thirlmere, and precipitous crags with scree slopes rise high towards Helvellyn and its neighbours in the east. To the west, the more modest heights of High Rigg and Low Rigg separate the Vale from the broad valley of the Naddle Beck. This valley carries the main Windermere to Keswick road, but the route has been carefully chosen to minimise contact with that often busy highway. St John's in the Vale church is a solid low Victorian (1845) rebuild of a much earlier church, well situated scenically but apparently remote from any likely congregation. John

St John's in The Vale: Castle Crag

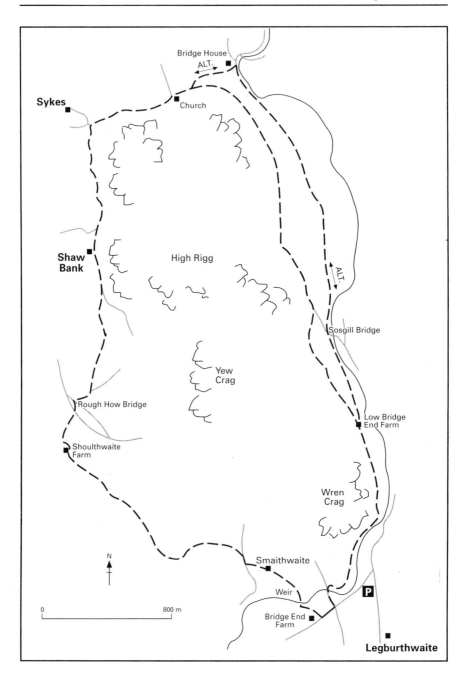

Richardson, (1817-1886), one of Lakeland's most celebrated dialect poets, had a long association with the church and with the former school adjacent. He is buried in the churchyard which is also noted for a restored old sundial.

Close to the car park, the hamlet of Legburthwaite has a small mission chapel..

Route

The car park/picnic area, with public conveniences, is not the easiest to find; look out for a small sign about 350 yards north of the Legburthwaite mission chapel. From the far end of the car park, go through a wooden gate and turn left along a lane leading to the main road. Turn right to cross the St. John's Beck and then immediately right over a ladder stile to follow the "footpath to St. John's in the Vale church". Keep left in a few yards (yellow arrow) taking a narrow path which rises over a shoulder and across a steep hillside with the beck close below. The path descends to pass below a shattered cliff with great boulders strewn below and the going underfoot improves as Blencathra comes into view ahead. Just before Low Bridge End Farm, angle to the left to pass behind the farm, then rising to traverse a plantation of conifers. Note the fine old packhorse bridge at Sosgill, below on the right.

A steady ascent, at a reasonable gradient, follows, down again past a long abandoned farmstead, and then up again on a wide grassy track towards the mini col, joining the surfaced road and turning left to reach the church inless than 100 yards.

(The alternative route to the church avoids most of the intermediate ups and downs by turning right, through a gate behind Low Bridge End farm, and then left to follow a path through the fields, alongside stone walls for about half of the distance and then bearing slightly left to head straight for Bridge House. Turn sharp left at Bridge House on to a path which climbs steeply in places, for 300 feet to the church. This route has the advantage of seeing Sosgill Bridge at close quarters).

From the church carry on over the top, as the road loses its surface and fine views to the North Western group of fells, with Grisedale Pike prominent, open up. Descend quite steeply towards Sykes Farm and turn left on the farm access road. Pass John Richardson's birthplace at Piper House and follow the road along the foot of the stony hillside for almost three quarters of a mile. After passing the last house, the road ends; head for a prominent finger post "public bridleway" which is, in fact, a narrow path winding across the hillside before dropping to a gate; bear right here towards the main road, reached via a "cut-off" roadway at Rough How Bridge. Take the lane to Shoulthwaite Farm, straight across the main road. Turn left, cross the beck, and pass behind the main farm buildings. Two gates give access to a pleasant woodland path. Just before joining a wider track, a notice states "long distance footpath to Dunmail". The track continues through and along the bottom edge of a large plantation, the great bulk of Helvellyn comes into view ahead, and a minor road is reached. Turn right for 50 yards and then left through a little gate, noting the Water Authority logo, passing rather dilapidated farm buildings en route to the St John's Beck. Here the choice is between stepping stones and a bridge, originally three arches of stone, but now the one remaining arch is disfigured by wooden accretions on each side. Follow the signs carefully to pass by Bridge End Farm and reach a minor road, with a good frontal view of Castle Rock across the valley. Turn left to the main road; cross with care to the gated lane opposite for the return to the car park.

31. Hartsop and Brotherswater

Walk: Hartsop Circular

Length: $4^1/_2$ miles.

Rise and Fall: 200 feet divided between several widely separated sections. Only one steep, but very short, gradient.

Underfoot: Good paths, narrow in places, with surfaced road through Hartsop village.

Car Parking: Official car park at Cow Bridge. Grid reference – 403133.

Ordnance Survey: "English Lakes, North Eastern area" 1:25000.

Description

Above Ullswater and Patterdale, the valley leading up to the Kirkstone Pass is one of Lakeland's loveliest and most interesting. To the west, Dovedale and Deepdale bite deeply into the massive Fairfield mountain complex; to the east, Hartsop Dodd and the slopes below Angle Tarn Pikes fall steeply to the valley floor, with plenty of evidence of the glacial processes which have played a large part in the final shaping of this valley. Brothers Water and the adjacent woodland contrast well with bare fellside on the one hand and with the neatly divided fields of most of the cultivated part of the valley floor on the other. The road south to Windermere climbs between the impressive flanks of Middle Dodd and Stony Cove Pike to reach the high and lonely Kirkstone Inn at the summit. Just 2 – 3 miles to the north, the villages of Patterdale and Glenridding, with Ullswater, offer a wide range of visitor facilities.

Stream at Hartsop

Route

The signposted car park is located where the Windermere to Patterdale road bends right and crosses the Goldrill Beck at Cow Bridge, opposite Hartsop village.

Cross the beck and, by the National Trust information board, go through the kissing gate, immediately turning very sharp right to follow the permissive footpath towards Patterdale. The path climbs a little and is narrow, but provides a good alternative to the road, which it follows closely alongside. Rejoin the road at a gate and cross straight over to take another permissive path signposted "Patterdale via Beckstones", largely along the top of the flood protection banking, to cross the valley. Place Fell, overlooking Ullswater, is prominent ahead. Cross the beck on a farm bridge and rise to join a bridleway, turning sharp right towards Hartsop. A good stony track now rises sufficiently to give fine views across the valley to the Fairfield group of mountains beyond. Above a rock on the left an old iron seat is strategically placed, while below on the right the old woodland is rich in hazel, covered in catkins through the bleak winter months.

The leaping falls and rapids of Angle Tarn Beck are soon in view, providing the first of many good picnic spots on this walk. Cross the stream by the bridge and follow the lane opposite, passing the reasonably discreet development of pine lodges at Hartsop Fold and the rather more obtrusive non-traditional farm buildings which follow. On reaching the road leading to Hartsop, turn left and ascend the meandering village street, looking out for the traditional spinning galleries on at least two of these lovely old buildings. (Should time or energy be short, or the weather have changed for the worse, the route can be shortened by turning right at the Hartsop road, and then left at the main road, to omit Hartsop. In extremis, a right turn at the main road provides a speedy return to the car park.)

To miss out Hartsop would, however, be a great pity and an amble to the car park at the top of the village is strongly recommended. From this car park take the gate at the far end and turn right to follow the "Pasture Beck" signpost; cross the stream and turn right again through a farm gate to return along the side of the stream. Keep right of the last house and then bear left into an unsurfaced lane which rises a little before

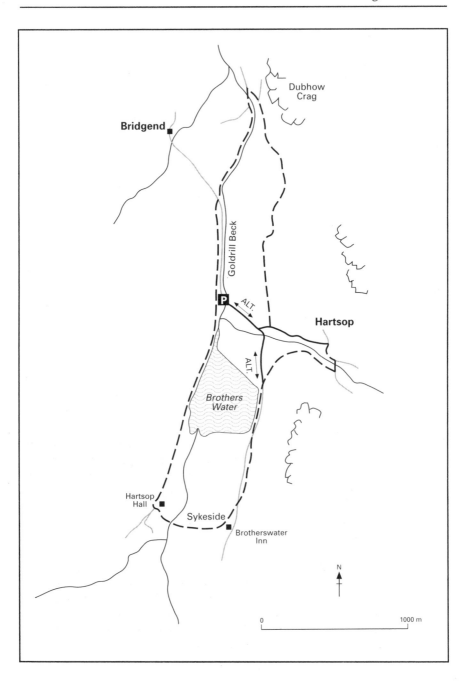

reaching the main road. Go straight across to a gate with a National Trust "Brothers Water" sign and bear left along a narrow, winding, lakeside footpath among the broken and gnarled old trees, with inviting spots for waterside picnics. At the far end of the lake the track climbs steeply for a few feet up to road level and then continues alongside the road to Sykeside and the Brothers Water Inn. Follow the Sykeside camping site drive through the middle of the site and continue across the valley to Hartsop Hall, one of Lakeland's oldest farmhouses. The track goes round the Hall, turning right across the back. From the Hall onwards a fine wide trackway heads straight back to the car park, terracing attractively through the woodland above Brothers Water with yet another shoreline, most easily accessible at the far end, tempting diversion from the serious business of walking. Allowing for ample stops and assuming a gentle pace, a half day would be appropriate for the full circuit; should time be pressing, a shortened version would result from initially heading along the road from the car park to Hartsop village and continuing the circuit from there.

Hartsop: 'Spinning gallery'

32. Ullswater

Walk: Glenridding to Howtown.

Length: 7½ miles.

Rise and Fall: Difficult to measure as the track rises and falls for most of the way, but a little more than 700 feet in total is near enough. No single rise is greater than 165 feet and, with the odd exception, gradients are easy.

Underfoot: Predominantly stony with some wet places. Three quarters of a mile is on or adjacent to the Patterdale to Glenridding road.

Car Parking: Car park at Glenridding steamer pier. Grid reference 390169. Alternatively, there are several roadside parking places; probably the best is by the "George Starkey Hut", Grid - reference 394161.

Ordnance Survey: "English Lakes, North Eastern area" 1:25000.

Description

After looking superficially at the map and then seeing the "lake shore footpath" sign and thinking of the return by "steamer", it would be easy to regard this walk as a gentle Sunday afternoon ramble in sandals. Don't!' Patterdale to Howtown is a surprisingly demanding walk, most of the way being well above the lake shore, rising and falling, sometimes abruptly, on a rough stony track, for more than 7 miles.

However, if you do have at least half a day to spare and can cope with the physical demands, don't hesitate. Join the hundreds of others who, daily in high season, find this excursion to be one of the most rewarding in Lakeland, combining what is arguably the most beautiful lake with views to Helvellyn and its neighbours. The return to Glenridding by "steamer" is pure delight. "Raven" and "Lady of the Lake" have plied their trade with considerable elegance on Ullswater for over one hundred years. Converted from steam to diesel in the 1930s, they operate daily between Glenridding, Howtown, and Pooley Bridge. In high season there are 8 sailings daily from Howtown to Glenridding, less in low season. Using the "steamer" for the return journey has the advantage of allowing leisurely admiration of the mountains at the head of-the lake after the hard work has been accomplished. There is no reason why this should not be reversed or, indeed, why a start should not be made at Howtown, where there is some car parking, should this be more convenient.

Ullswater

Route

From the car park at the steamer pier, look for a small gate and take the path cutting diagonally across the large grassy area to reach the road. There is a refreshment hut by the roadside and public conveniences are situated 200 yards to the right. Turn left at the road and proceed for three quarters of a mile towards Patterdale. By the nearside of the

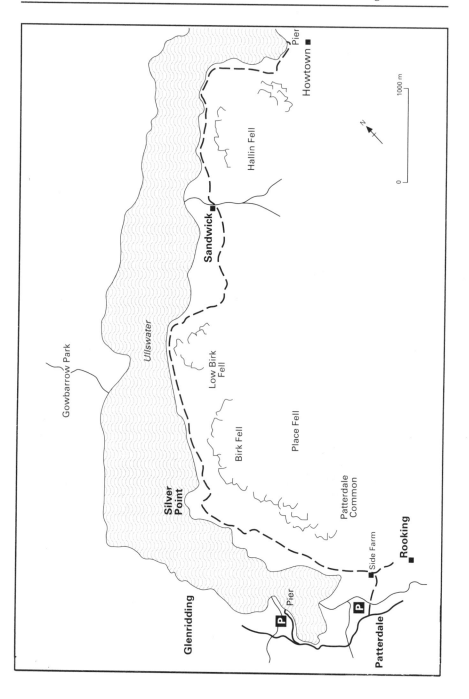

"George Starkey Hut", a substantial stone building set back from the road, turn left into a lane which crosses the valley to Side Farm, where light refreshments may be purchased. Turn left, soon passing through woodland, largely of mature sycamore. Beyond the woodland, the views are of Glenridding, with the steamer pier and the Ullswater Hotel prominent and the remains of the former Greenside lead mine well up the valley behind. Above on the right is the considerable bulk of Place Fell, around whose rough flanks our path skirts for several miles. The track rises steadily above a camping field; where there is a choice of route bear left downhill to keep between Silver Crag and the lake. (The alternative may be used, but more ascent is required). As the path bends to the right above Silver Point, views along the lake to the north east open up. The subsequent descent to the lake shore is through woodland dominated by birch, one of the truly native trees of the district.

From the lake shore the next rise is the longest and steepest of the walk. Further up and down is rewarded by a good view of Scalehow Force, a modest waterfall. Cross a footbridge, pass a stone barn and, where the track divides at a grassy area, keep left by the wall, downhill to a surfaced road. Blocking the way ahead is Hallin Fell, which can be passed on either side but the route using the road to the right is higher and steeper than the lakeside path. So, turn left at the road and then right at a "footpath to Howtown" sign, cross Sandwick Beck by the bridge, and continue to the lake shore, by Hallinhag Wood, where there are good picnic spots. As the path bends to the right, the view now includes the far end of the lake, including Pooley Bridge and shapely Dunmallard Hill adjacent. Below is Howtown steamer pier, with the hamlet of the same name 300 yards inland. Turn left down a flight of steps towards the lake and keep close to the shore, following the signs, to reach the pier. There is a timetable inside the shelter building.

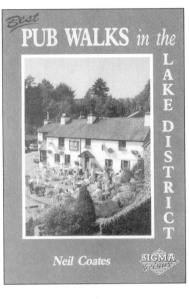

BEST PUB WALKS IN THE LAKE DISTRICT

Neil Coates

This, the longest-established (and best-researched) pub walks book for the Lakes, is amazingly wide-ranging, with an emphasis on quality of walks and the real ale rewards that follow! *£6.95*

LAKELAND CHURCH WALKS

Peter Donaghy and John Laidler

Nominated for Lakeland Book of The Year, 2002 – and with a foreword by Simon Jenkins of *The Times*. 30 detailed circular walks ranging from 3½ to 12 miles with alternative shorter options, each starting from a noteworthy church. *£8.95*

MORE TEA SHOP WALKS IN THE LAKE DISTRICT

Norman and June Buckley

Leisurely rambles in fine scenery with the bonus of afternoon tea or morning coffee – or both – in a variety of tea shops from tiny cafés to stately homes. Crossing both the central regions and the lesser-known fringe areas, their 25 easy-going, circular walks range from 2 to 9 miles. *£6.95*

WALKS IN ANCIENT LAKELAND

Robert Harris

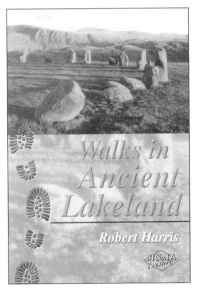

A collection of 24 fascinating ancient Lakeland circular walks ranging in length from 2 to 10 miles, each visiting sites and monuments from the Neolithic and Bronze ages, linked where possible with ancient trackways. All walks are accompanied by sketch maps, and the author's intricate hand-drawn sketches. *£6.95*

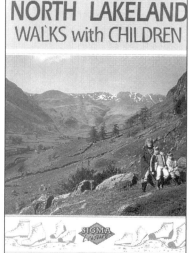

NORTH LAKELAND WALKS WITH CHILDREN

Mary Welsh; illustrations by Christine Isherwood

"It has been great fun speaking to children I have met on the walks and listening to what they have to say" says Mary Welsh, author. Her refreshing, enthusiastic attitude is reflected in her book, written specifically with the needs, entertainment and safety of children in mind. Perfect for parents of reluctant walkers. *£7.95*

SOUTH LAKELAND WALKS WITH CHILDREN

Nick Lambert

The companion guide for complete coverage – children really can enjoy walking with the help of Nick Lambert's guide. He seems to have thought of everything to keep both parents and children happy – clear directions take you along 20 varied, well-maintained paths which can be tackled by even the youngest family members. *£6.95*

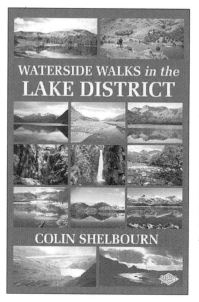

WATERSIDE WALKS IN THE LAKE DISTRICT

Colin Shelbourn

A unique compilation of 25 walks around and alongside a selection of the many water features to be found in this favourite walking area - lakes, tarns, becks, rivers and waterfalls. Ranging from 1 to 16 km, from gentle strolls to more strenuous hikes there are suitable walks for all age groups. Each walk includes information about parking, the length of the walk, a clear map to guide you, the level of difficulty, entertaining background information and many beautiful photographs. *£7.95*